CITYSPOTS
BRUS

CITYSPOTS

WHAT'S IN YOUR GUIDEBOOK?

Independent authors Impartial up-to-date information from our travel experts who meticulously source local knowledge.

Experience Thomas Cook's 165 years in the travel industry and guidebook publishing enriches every word with expertise you can trust.

Travel know-how Contributions by thousands of staff around the globe, each one living and breathing travel.

Editors Travel-publishing professionals, pulling everything together to craft a perfect blend of words, pictures, maps and design.

You, the traveller We deliver a practical, no-nonsense approach to information, geared to how you really use it.

CITYSPOTS
BRUSSELS

Ryan Levitt

Thomas Cook

Written by Ryan Levitt
Original photography by Neil Setchfield
Cover photo (Atomium) © The Travel Library Limited/www.photolibrary.com
Series design based on an original concept by Studio 183 Limited

Produced by Cambridge Publishing Management Limited
Project Editor: Catherine Burch
Layout: Paul Queripel
Maps: PC Graphics
Transport map: © Communicarta Limited

Published by Thomas Cook Publishing
A division of Thomas Cook Tour Operations Limited
Company Registration No. 1450464 England
PO Box 227, Unit 18, Coningsby Road
Peterborough PE3 8SB, United Kingdom
email: books@thomascook.com
www.thomascookpublishing.com
+ 44 (0) 1733 416477
ISBN-13: 978-1-84157-746-3

First edition © 2007 Thomas Cook Publishing
Text © 2007 Thomas Cook Publishing
Maps © 2007 Thomas Cook Publishing
Series/Project Editor: Kelly Anne Pipes
Production/DTP: Steven Collins

Printed and bound in Spain by GraphyCems

CONTENTS

SYMBOLS KEY

The following symbols are used throughout this book:

ⓐ address   ⓣ telephone   ⓦ website address
🕒 opening times   Ⓝ public transport connections   ❶ important

The following symbols are used on the maps:

𝒊	information office	O	city
✈	airport	O	large town
➕	hospital	○	small town
⏱	police station	═	motorway
🚌	bus station	▬	main road
🚆	railway station	▬	minor road
Ⓜ	metro	—	railway
✝	cathedral		
❶	numbers denote featured cafés & restaurants		

Hotels and restaurants are graded by approximate price as follows:

£ budget   ££ mid-range   £££ expensive

▶ *Ornate guild houses overlook the Grand Place*

INTRODUCING
Brussels

Introduction

Brussels has always had a bit of a boring reputation. Grey-clad Eurocrats creating annoying legislation, rain-drenched days, bizarre linguistic issues – it's not exactly the picture of a perfect holiday.

Well, it's time to banish your misconceptions and embrace the new Brussels, a city of culinary masterpieces, hot nights of clubbing, art treasures and cutting-edge performance.

Situated just over two hours from London by train, and linked with almost every regional airport in the UK and Ireland, Brussels offers easy connections for those looking for a convenient and intriguing short-break destination. And those with financial limitations can pack their days with a variety of free sights that take in the best of the city.

Grand Place is the heart of the Lower Town. Once described by Victor Hugo (author of *Les Miserables*) as the most beautiful square in Europe, this collection of guild houses in the Italian baroque style is simply breathtaking. But that's not all there is to see in this historic quarter. There's also the Manneken Pis, a fountain of a peeing boy that is considered a symbol of the city.

Over in Upper Town are royal sights and inspiring galleries, including the newest addition to the scene, a fascinating gallery devoted to the history of musical instruments.

And if you thought that the city was all about European culture, you'd be mistaken. A vibrant African population in the ethnically diverse neighbourhood of Ixelles offers up great restaurants, markets, bars and clubs for visitors looking for something out of the ordinary.

So forget about what you might have heard about Brussels in the past. This city is sprouting with a new vibe and is ready to welcome you with a friendly smile and a pint of one of its amazing beers. The drink alone should be enough to convince you to visit.

● *There's something to see in the Grand Place all the year round*

When to go

Brussels is worth visiting at any time of year, since there is always plenty to do and see. For many, it is during the summer period when the city really comes alive. At this time of the year live music concerts take over city squares, open-air film screenings draw the masses and the population explodes with excitement.

If what goes on in the city itself is not enough, then head off to any of the nearby cities. The winding cobbled streets of Leuven, the military fascination of Waterloo, and the fast fashion of Antwerp are all enticing in their own right and well worth taking time away from the Belgian capital.

SEASONS & CLIMATE

The climate of Brussels is similar to what you might find in London: often overcast, damp for much of the winter, yet sunny and bright for long periods during the summer. Year-round temperatures seldom drop below 0°C (32°F) or rise above 25°C (77°F).

If you don't mind the chill, winter is a pleasant time to visit for avoiding the tourist crowds. Snow is seldom a consideration, and the winter fogs actually add an atmosphere that make you feel as if you're in a period film.

In the early spring, the meaning of the old saying 'April showers bring May flowers' becomes clear – but in this city's case the showers can often stretch into June. When summer finally does arrive, the thermometer hovers around the mid-20s°C (70s°F) with occasional heat waves that usually last no longer than a couple of days. Street activity blossoms during this period as the long days and outdoor cafés create a buzzing atmosphere.

The best season to visit for in terms of, crowds and weather is autumn. The buzz of the streets may be gone, but there are still plenty of things to see and do – and the threat of rain is greatly reduced.

○ *The famous Carpet of Flowers blooms in the Grand Place*

ANNUAL EVENTS

In Brussels and the surrounding region there are many more events than can be mentioned here. That said, the tourist offices for Brussels and the surrounding region can provide a full list. ❶ Note that exact dates of events may change from year to year – so check first. ⓦ www.bitc.be gives a comprehensive calendar of events.

March

Brussels International Festival of Fantastic Film Two-week film festival dedicated to horror and sci-fi film. Prepare yourself for the gore! Always a lot of fun. Side events such as body-painting exhibits and fetish shows go along for the ride. The final event is a Vampire Ball. Tickets sell out well in advance and you'll only get in if you're wearing a killer costume. ⓦ www.bifff.org. Dates vary.

May

Jazz Marathon Three days of non-stop jazz take over almost all the bars, clubs and stages in the city. Shuttle buses run between the major venues. Each year more than 250,000 people come to listen to the music. So book your hotel room well in advance. ⓦ www.brusselsjazzmarathon.be. Dates vary.

June

Battle of Waterloo See the epic battle that destroyed Napoléon recreated on the field where the tides turned against him. Re-enactments are only held every five years. The next event is scheduled for 2010 ⓦ www.culture-espaces.com/waterloo

Festival of Flanders/Festival of Wallonia Two festivals, two languages, one big celebration of culture. Classical music is the core focus of both festivals with concerts planned throughout the country. ⓦ www.festivaldewallonie.be/ & www.festival.be

July
National Day National celebration featuring pageantry, military displays and royal family sightings, held every year on 21 July.

December
Le Marché de Noël Brussels' Christmas market packed with wooden stalls selling *Glühwein* (or 'mulled wine'), wooden toys and Christmas ornaments runs along the road from Grand Place to Place Ste-Catherine, ending at an open-air skating rink.
ⓦ www.plaisirsdhiver.be

PUBLIC HOLIDAYS
New Year's Day 1 January
Easter Sunday March/April
Easter Monday March/April
Labour Day 1 May
Ascension Day 6th Sunday after Easter
Pentecostal Whit Monday 7th Monday after Easter
Belgian National Day 21 July
Assumption 15 August
All Saints' Day 1 November
Armistice Day 11 November
Christmas Day 25 December

Ommegang

Re-live the Golden Age of the city by joining in the fun of Ommegang. This stately procession re-enacts a similar event which honoured the entry of the Emperor Charles V into the city in 1549 with festivities lasting for three days. Locals dress up as nobles, guildsmen, jesters and any other random 16th-century resident they can think of.

The procession can be made on horseback or on foot and runs for about 2 km (just over 1 mile) from the Upper Town to the Lower Town, ending at Grand Place. A grandstand is set up allowing views of the jousting tournament, horse parade and stilt fighting. However, tickets must be booked well in advance. Seats usually sell out about two months prior to the day. If you don't want to fight the crowds, go instead to the cafés at the Place du Grand Sablon where you can watch the start of the parade. It's not as visually exciting or as much fun, but you'll get to see everything without the jostling or ticket expense.

The procession is held on the first Thursday of July. However, the party atmosphere lasts through the weekend. Ommegang literally means 'walk around' in Flemish, and that's essentially all you do. Walk around the streets in the procession, walk around from bar to bar, walk around to see your friends – it's a very social and welcoming event. If ever you wanted to see Belgians dissolve their traditionally frosty exterior, then now is the time to visit.

Kids love Ommegang because of the medieval re-enactments, colourful garb, flying banners and displays of horsemanship. Adults love what happens after dark when the entire city turns into the scene of the nation's biggest knees-up. As you'd expect, hotel rooms need to be reserved well in advance.

ⓐ Grand Place ⓣ 02 512 1961 ⓦ www.ommegang-brussels.be
ⓘ Tickets must be pre-booked.

🔺 *Ommegang: fun to watch, even more fun to join in!*

History

The city of Brussels was first mentioned in a 7th-century manuscript. It is thought that the name Brussels came from the Flemish word *Broekzele* (or 'marshland'), as the original foundations of the city were on an island in the River Senne.

Historically, the founding date of the city is attributed to the year 580 when Saint Géry is said to have built a chapel somewhere in the region of the Lower Town. By the 9th century, the town had grown into a prosperous mercantile community ruled by the Franks who overtook the region following the fall of the Roman Empire.

City walls protected the citizens of Brussels until the 13th century, when population growth put pressure on the town. Craftsmen moved to the city to assist with construction and trade began to boom. Fabrics and textile making were the chief money-making industries causing neighbouring forces to note and admire the region's wealth.

At the end of the 14th century, the city was invaded by the Count of Flanders, forcing new fortifications to be built around the city. These fortifications follow the path of the Petit Ring. However, none of the original gates exist today.

A key royal marriage brought the city under the rule of Burgundy, and the city was proclaimed capital of Burgundy in the 1430s. The result was a boom in revenue and trade. This period of peace lasted until 1466 when another royal marriage allowed the Habsburgs to capture control of the city. Locals hated the Habsburgs and the capital was taken away from them for a period of about 40 years.

Prosperity reigned during this period until the Reformation divided the city, triggering riots between Catholics and Protestants. The battles continued until the Spanish were defeated by the English (Protestants).

More empires fought for control over this strategically important city. First came the French in 1695 which resulted in the destruction of the Grand Place. The guilds soon rebuilt all the houses and the badly-damaged town hall. Next came the Austrians in the early 18th century. Austrian rule ensued and eventually bankrupted the city coffers as the War of Austrian Succession stripped the city of almost all its assets.

Following the French Revolution, the working classes began to revolt against the demands of the Austrian throne. Their struggles resulted in a War of Independence which established an independent nation in 1830.

The 20th century continued to be eventful. The city blossomed with the rise of art nouveau, only for the Germans to occupy their fledgling state during both world wars despite the country's stated neutrality.

Today, Brussels is the heart of Europe; home to both the European Union and NATO, and a leading force in politics and business.

Lifestyle

As they live in the heart of northern Europe, and have a strong tradition of trade and travel, Belgians exhibit characteristics commonly associated with neighbouring nations – and combine those traits into something truly unique.

Say the word 'Europe' and residents will be the first to complain about rising housing costs, expenditure on public services, overcrowding and traffic. On the quiet, however, it's a different matter, as Belgians love the idea of being considered the unofficial capital country of the EU. Due to years of invasion, Belgians truly do represent Europe. Where one local will exhibit Nordic features that recall Scandinavian and Dutch influences in the country, another will look almost Spanish – yet both will be Belgian through and through.

TRADITIONS AND ETIQUETTE

Belgians have a reputation for following unspoken northern European codes of practice to mind their own business and keep their front doors firmly shut. This belief may be partly true. Some people say that trying to prise an invitation out of a Belgian to visit their family home is a bit like trying to find Willy Wonka's golden ticket; but get them out of the house and locals are just as generous, exciting and talkative as the next person. Their apparent habit of zealously protecting their privacy is somewhat rooted in history.

The one thing that binds Belgians together, and is a constant source of discussion and debate, is the separation of Dutch-speaking Flanders from French-speaking Wallonia. Like a couple who have been married too long (yet can't live without each other), the two linguistically divided halves of the country are constantly at odds. Yet, when the country was formed in 1830, these two communities elected to stay together rather than run the risk of independence. Deep down, both the Flemish and the Walloons have read their history books and know that they are better off together.

● *Place Ste-Catherine is a lovely place to unwind*

Culture

Belgians are big supporters of the arts, both contemporary and classic. This is not one of those countries whose people will only attend performances of old favourites or historically important plays. Rather, residents eagerly await cutting-edge modern dance and contemporary music with a fervour unmatched anywhere else in Europe.

Classical music

While the nobility of Belgium haven't always been huge fans, classical music has thrived in Brussels. Major works by such leading lights as Stravinsky and Bartók premiered in this city, and the Théâtre de la Monnaie is experiencing a revival under the solid new direction of Japanese maestro Kazushi Ono.

Because Belgium is a bilingual nation, public funding is stretched to its limits. For every Flemish company there must be an equivalent French version. The end result is that organisations with promise fall by the wayside as they struggle to keep up with financial obligations. Despite this fact, concertgoers have reason to rejoice as world-class festivals revive their spirits every May in the form of the Concours Musical International Reine Elisabeth de Belgique (Queen Elisabeth International Music Competition of Belgium). Founded in 1937, this annual festival has a rotating schedule concentrating on violin, piano, composition and vocal performance. The final gala is always sold out, drawing an audience from across the linguistic divide (Ⓦ www.cmireb.be/).

⬥ *You'll love the famous Toone Theatre (see page 73)*

Art & galleries

While locals are huge consumers of contemporary art, they tend to avoid the galleries of Belgium in favour of the more noted spaces of London, New York and Berlin. This refusal to purchase local work isn't due to a lack of talent. Rather, it's because there are so few commercial galleries in the city. If you are determined to check out what's on offer, plan your visit around the Brussels Art Fair held each spring (Ⓦ www.artexis.com/artbrussels).

Theatre & dance

Most theatrical performance in Brussels is in Flemish or French. For the best options, check out the programming at the Royal Flemish Theatre or Théâtre National. For experimental work, go instead to the Beursschouwburg (Ⓦ www.beursschouwburg.be), and mix with the hip and happening audience. English language theatre troupes abound in Brussels but strictly at an amateur level. Companies to look out for include the American Theater Company, English Theatre Brussels, Brussels Light Opera Company and Brussels Shakespeare Society.

Dance-wise, Brussels leads the world as an innovator and producer of influential modern choreography. Classical work may be the speciality of the renowned Royal Ballet of Flanders (Ⓦ www.koninkljikballetvanvlaanderen.be), but it's the cutting-edge work of companies such as the Rosas company under the direction of Anne Teresa de Keersmaeker (Ⓦ www.rosas.be) and Frédéric Flamand's Charleroi Danse that truly excites and energises.

▶ *The legendary, Belgian-created, Tintin and Snowy*

Shopping

In Belgium, each city has its specialities and treats. Antwerp is known for its high fashion, and Gent for its lace. In Brussels, it's all about the food. Sinfully sweet chocolate. Organic meats and vegetables. Creamy cheeses and bottles of delicious beer. For truly exotic offerings, the streets of Ixelles offer plenty of opportunities for shopping sensations; otherwise explore the one-off offerings of the shops of the historic Lower Town for the finest in food and drink.

While shopping centres aren't a standard feature of the city's streets, there are covered arcades known as *galeries*, very similar to the arcades of London. These quiet mini-malls boast unique boutiques of designer fashions and speciality goods that are high on price and quality. The best-known galerie is the Galerie St-Hubert located slightly northeast of Grand Place.

For true treasures, head down to the Place du Jeu de Balle in the heart of the working-class neighbourhood of Les Marolles where a flea market has been held since 1873. The market beckons shoppers every single day of the week with its collection of jewels and junk. You'll have to hunt long and hard for finds – but when you strike gold, you'll experience a high that's difficult to match.

If you prefer your shopping experiences to be less stressful, go instead to the more salubrious antiques centre at Passage 125 on Rue Blaes. This large warehouse is tucked in between a slew of restored furniture shops and offers the collections of more than 25 top-notch dealers, all of whom can arrange worldwide shipping.

⬤ *Some things are not meant to last*

If you're looking for big names, fear not. With so many Eurocrat shoppers and their spouses in town, you can guarantee that there is a lot of Gucci and Versace to go around. Avenue Louise and the Boulevard du Waterloo are the streets to head for if your idea of shopping comes with a six-figure price tag.

USEFUL SHOPPING PHRASES

What time do the shops open/close?
A quelle heure ouvrent/ferment les magasins?
Ah kehlur oovr/fehrm leh mahgazhang?

How much is this?
C'est combien?
Cey combyahng?

Can I try this on?
Puis-je essayer ceci?
Pweezh ehssayeh cerssee?

My size is...
Ma taille (clothes)/
ma pointure (shoes) est ...
Mah tie/mah pooahngtewr ay ...

I'll take this one, thank you
Je prends celui-ci/celle-ci merci
*Zher prahng serlweesi/
sehlsee mehrsee*

Eating & drinking

Belgium has more Michelin-starred chefs per capita than any other country on the planet. Combine that with the seemingly endless expense accounts of the Eurocrat brigade and what you have is a dining scene that is simply beyond compare. Belgian food is a combination of French cuisine – often covered in sauce – fresh seafood and hearty German and Dutch fare.

Locals are picky when it comes to ingredients, as the nation's mercantile past has brought the flavours of the world to them, and residents know their culinary stuff. Not for them the tasteless fruit and veg of a typical British supermarket. Flavour is where it's at, meaning that seasonality and freshness are prized above all.

Food has been a valued part of daily life for centuries. Belgians have long had a reputation for being hard-working, yet keen to celebrate when the occasion arises. The best reward for them after a long day at the office is a well-prepared meal – and they will work long and hard to ensure that only the best is dished up.

The cuisine of Brussels is heavily influenced by the flavours of its regions. Fresh seafood from the coast, game from the Ardennes, rich sauces from Wallonia and, of course, beer.

RESTAURANT CATEGORIES
Price ratings given in this book are based on the cost of a main course at dinner, including tax and tip.

£ up to €10   ££ €10–€20   £££ above €20

What really differentiates the cooking of Brussels from that of other regions of Belgium is its variety. Nowhere else has such a large ethnic community offering the flavours of the Congo, Asia and India.

⬤ *You can't beat a cold Belgian beer*

The mussels of Brussels no longer come from Belgian waters. The best varieties come from nearby Dutch ports and many signs will advertise this fact. This is due to the heavy pollution off the Belgian shore.

Other seafood varieties to look out for include oysters, small, sweet-tasting shrimp from the North Sea and eels from the rural canals that dot the countryside. The spicy cocktail sauces and tartare sauces that are often served with British and American dishes aren't commonly served with Belgian fish and seafood, so if you really want the added condiments, you'll have to ask for them.

As for game and meat, these ingredients are best found in restaurants that specialise in cuisine from the Ardennes. This wild forest produces tasty venison, wild boar and pheasant. Rich flavours are this area's speciality, often to the detriment of simpler beef and chicken dishes. The shortage of large areas of grazing land means that beef isn't a speciality of Belgium, however, you will find it imported and on most menus.

FISH & CHIPS BELGIAN STYLE

You don't have to spend a fortune to enjoy a good meal. The most famous and fast dish in the country is *moules frites*, which is typically a bowl of steamed mussels in either a clear, herbed broth or tomato-based sauce served up with crisp *frites* (or 'chips' by any other name) and a dollop of mayonnaise. You can find this dish at almost every café and restaurant in the city – and each will keep their sauce ingredients a closely guarded secret.

World-famous Belgian beer washes the food down. There are about 120 breweries producing 500 types of beer in a dozen styles with 50 sub-categories available in Belgium. A good café or restaurant will serve a minimum of 10 different brands and varieties. Ask your bartender for a recommendation if you don't know which variety to try. You'll often find that beer is also an integral ingredient of the dish you are ordering for dinner.

❶ To help make your decisions, consider a day trip to nearby Leuven – home to the famous Stella Artois brewery. This massive factory offers tours of the facilities in addition to tastings of its product (see page 124).

USEFUL DINING PHRASES

I would like a table for ... people
Je voudrais une table pour ... personnes
Zher voodray ewn tabl poor ... pehrson

May I have the bill, please?
L'addition, s'il vous plaît!
Laddyssyawng, sylvooplay!

Waiter/waitress!
Monsieur/Mademoiselle, s'il vous plaît?
M'sewr/madmwahzel, sylvooplay!

Does it have meat in it?
Est-ce que ce plat contient de la viande?
Essker ser plah kontyang der lah veeahngd?

Where is the toilet please?
Où sont les toilettes, s'il vous plaît?
Oo sawng leh twahlaitt, sylvooplay?

Entertainment & nightlife

Brussels may be a hard-working town but it likes to play hard too. Locals think nothing of spending an evening sipping local brews in a bar, especially when they have such a variety of beers to choose from. City bars don't have an official closing time and many stay open until the wee hours of the morning. Take advantage of this situation by pulling up a barstool and chatting to the locals who call these drinking dens their home from home. It is during these conversations that you truly capture the spirit of Brussels.

CINEMA

Cinema is another favourite pastime. You can even see how the industry was built up during its early days at the fascinating Musée du Cinema, where there are regular nightly screenings of silent movies complete with piano music accompaniment. Another popular option is the weekend open-air screenings sponsored by the Nova cinema during the summer months where quirky classics are showcased to picnicking residents at sundown. Check local listings for details.

MUSIC

While there aren't many local bands with an international reputation, there is still a thriving local live music scene. It takes a lot for a local band to generate a following, as there are no laws that ensure Belgian bands will get airplay on local radio stations. There's everything from Jacques Brel-style *chanteurs* through cutting-edge electro available on any given evening –

● *Enjoy live jazz at the l'Archiduc jazz café*

but don't go expecting the selection of a London or even a Manchester. For big names, there are two large-scale venues that draw the crowds: The Forest National and the slightly more intimate Ancienne Belgique.

As the home of the saxophone, Belgium is well known for its jazz venues. The now-ancient Toot Thielemans and the late great Django Reinhardt both cut their teeth in the clubs of Brussels. Join the throngs at the annual Jazz Marathon Festival, which takes over hundreds of venues every May (see page 12). It's a great opportunity to dabble between bars and listen to performers both amateur and professional.

World music is another speciality of the city, served up in the bars and clubs of the ethnic neighbourhood of Ixelles. A night in this happening community will expose you to African, Asian and South American sounds with a strong focus on the music of Belgium's former colony, the Congo. The biggest festival of world sounds is the Couleur Café festival in June at the Tour et Taxis.

CLUBS

For a truly memorable evening, you should go clubbing. While the clubs of the capital aren't as 'wow' as those in the musically edgy cities of Antwerp or Leuven, there's still plenty to keep you occupied. The country considers itself to be the founding father of European techno and welcomes a plethora of international DJs to back up that claim.

The headquarters of this movement is the legendary club Fuse. At first glance you might find there isn't much to look at in this hangar-style space, but it's been at the forefront of musical styles for over a decade now and continues to welcome in the masses (even if there is more of a suburban vibe these days).

For the best nights out, avoid the branded clubs and go instead to the one-off nights at venues scattered throughout the city in alternative dance spaces. Recyclart is a great example of such an evening with its mission to showcase up-and-coming acts and DJs.

● *For something a bit different, try an evening at Recyclart*

Sport & relaxation

CYCLING

When it comes to keeping fit and exercising, Belgians are a
hearty lot. Daily activity is a way of life for locals – and not
simply due to a desire to keep the body trim and toned. Cycling
and jogging are the most common methods of getting the
heart pumping due to the flat topography of the city.

If you want to get on a bike to explore points in the city that
are further afield, then it is possible to rent a bicycle on a daily
or weekend rate. Prices range from €13 for a day.

Pro Vélo ② Rue de Londres 15 ① 02 502 7355 ⓦ www.provelo.org
🕐 10.00–18.00 Mon–Fri, Nov–Mar; 10.00–18.00 Mon–Fri,
13.00–14.00 Sat & Sun, Apr–Oct ⓜ Metro: Trône

GOLF

Space limitations mean that large-scale athletic centres and
golf courses are a rarity. Despite this, golf remains a popular
pastime, with many Eurocrats using the links as an extension of
their networking sessions. As the Eurocrats can spend, spend,
spend, fees on local courses can be out of the affordable range
for average tourists – especially during peak weekend periods.
Call ahead to determine costs and tee time possibilities.

A good bet for beginners is the Golf Club Academy and
Training Centre close to the Fôret de Soignes, where you can
book lessons from pros and training sessions. Contact the
Academy for packages that include hotel rooms and multiple
day passes if you want to make a full holiday out of your golfing
experience.

Royal Golf Club of Belgium ⓐ Château de Ravenstein, Tervuren
ⓣ 02 767 5801 ⓦ www.ravenstein.be
Brabantse Golf Club ⓐ Steenwagenstraat 11, Melsbrook
ⓣ 03 751 8205
Golf Club Academy and Training Centre ⓐ Chaussée de la Hulpe
53a ⓣ 02 672 2222

ICE SKATING

In winter, ice skating becomes the pastime of choice and there is
no better (or more magical) place to enjoy it than in Ste
Catherine. In the lead-up to Christmas, the Place du Marché-
aux-Poissons becomes an outdoor skating rink where you can
rent skates to glide past the historic architecture. Skates cost
around €5 to rent. Combine it with a shopping trip at the
Christmas market for a full seasonal experience.

● *Ice skating on Grand Place*

Accommodation

Brussels has plenty of hotel rooms due to its function as the unofficial capital of the EU. While this means you can often find deals, it also puts strong focus on business travelling needs – so some hotels are a bit lacking in character.

The basic rule of thumb is that properties in the Lower Town will be more expensive at weekends and designed for tourists, while hotels in the EU Quarter, outside the Petit Ring and close to the parliament buildings in Upper Town, will cater for those with large expense accounts.

Despite this wealth of accommodation, summers can get busy (especially at weekends), so if you are planning a visit around this time, it is best to book ahead.

If your visit to Brussels is a spur-of-the-moment decision, then consider booking your room through the Brussels Tourist Information Office at ⓐ Rue Marché aux Herbes 63 (ⓣ 02 504 0390). Alternatively, book through Resotel (ⓣ 02 779 3939 ⓦ www.belgiumhospitality.com). Very often, their rates are better than those provided by any other booking method available.

PRICE RATING

Hotels in Belgium are graded according to a star system running from one star for a cheap guesthouse to five stars for a luxurious property with numerous facilities.
The ratings in this book are per double or twin room per night.

£ up to €75   ££ €75–€150   £££ over €150

HOTELS

Monty Hotel £–££ Inconveniently located but high on design sense, this great hotel features interior fittings from some of today's hottest designers (Philippe Starck, Ingo Maurer, etc.) and a welcoming atmosphere. Too bad it's so far from the city centre. Good for the sights at Parc du Cinquantenaire. ⓐ Boulevard Brand Whitlock 101 ❶ 02 734 5636 ⓦ www.monty-hotel.be ⓝ Metro: Montgomery

Noga ££ A nice choice if you want comfort on a budget. Noga offers colourful, clean rooms that are convenient for your explorations. All rooms have ensuite showers. ⓐ Rue du Béguinage 38 ❶ 02 218 6763 ⓦ www.nogahotel.com ⓝ Metro: Ste-Catherine

Stanhope ££–£££ If you can get a deal, this hotel is often a great place to rest your head. As the building comprises three classic town homes, there is a real home-from-home feel to the property. Rooms feature luxurious amenities such as marble bathrooms and canopied beds. Each room is different, so be sure to look at a few options before you make your final selection. ⓐ Rue du Commerce 9 ❶ 02 506 9111 ⓦ www.summithotels.com ⓝ Metro: Trône

Hotel Amigo £££ Check in here if you truly want to impress the one you're with. Once a prison, the Amigo is now the hottest spot in town for visiting celebs and minor royals. Acres of marble, the finest silks, crisp linens – it's all here in abundance. Service is uniformly spectacular. Magritte and Tintin prints in

⬥ *Hotel Amigo offers luxury at the heart of the city*

the rooms add a Belgian touch. ❸ Rue de l'Amigo 1–3
❶ 02 547 4747 ❿ www.hotelamigo.com ❻ Metro: Gare Centrale

Le Dixseptième £££ Once the home of the Spanish ambassador,
this restored hotel dating from the 17th century is designed
with comfort in mind. It has a traditional style, complete with
exposed beams, overstuffed suede sofas and windows that
overlook a peaceful interior courtyard. ❸ Rue de la Madeleine 25
❶ 02 517 1717 ❿ www.ledixseptieme.be ❻ Metro: Gare Centrale

Dorint £££ A typical Eurocrat business hotel, this property is
packed out during the week with mid-scale politicians drawn by
its location convenient for all the European Parliament
buildings. While the artwork gives the property a bit of a funky
edge, it's still a business hotel when all is said and done. At
weekends, when the politicians jet home, prices can drop to
below €80 a night. ❸ Boulevard Charlemagne 11–19 ❶ 02 231
0909 ❻ Metro: Schuman

GUESTHOUSES & B&BS
Les Bleuts £ This kitsch-filled hotel is packed with bizarre antiques
that will make you feel like you're in the home of a true eccentric –
and you'd be right. A non-smoking and silence rule is strictly
enforced by the slightly out-to-lunch owner. But the quirky
character of the place makes up for the overall weirdness.
❸ Rue Berckmans 124 ❶ 02 534 3983 ❻ Metro: Hôtel des Monnaies

La Vielle Lanterne £ Small family-run B&B overlooking the
Manneken Pis. Each of the six rooms has an ensuite shower.

Furnishings are basic but clean – and you can't beat the breakfast in bed included in the room price. ⓐ Rue des Grands Carmes 29 ⓣ 02 512 7494 Ⓝ Metro: Bourse

HOSTELS

Centre Vincent Van Gogh £ This massive youth hostel is the largest cheap sleep option in town. Often full with school groups, it can become fully booked months in advance. Well stocked with games and bright common rooms, it's a clean and simple place to rest your head – so long as you don't mind sharing with gaggles of pre-teens on a class trip. ⓐ Rue Traversière 8 ⓣ 02 217 0158 Ⓝ Metro: Botanique

Sleep Well £ Bright and friendly youth hostel with great transport links. Singles, doubles, triples and dorms are on offer. Bathrooms are shared. Sheets cost extra. Spend a little more for a room in the Star section if you want the luxury of an ensuite bathroom. ⓐ Rue du Damier 23 ⓣ 02 218 5050 Ⓦ www.sleepwell.be Ⓝ Metro: Rogier

THE BEST OF BRUSSELS

Brussels offers much to entertain, interest and please the senses, and is a great place to visit for a short weekend break filled with fine art, chocolate and beer.

TOP 10 ATTRACTIONS

- **Grand Place** Brussels' main square, described by Victor Hugo as the most beautiful square in Europe (see page 61).

- **Manneken Pis** He may just be a boy having a wee, but to many he's the symbol of a nation (see page 64).

- **Musée Horta** A graceful example of the contribution to art nouveau made by Belgium's favourite architect (see page 97).

- **Atomium** This super-size model of an atom remains a popular tourist destination. The views from the top are superb (see page 88).

- **Parc du Cinquantenaire** The city's favourite green space built by Léopold II (see page 92).

- **Musée Royaux des Beaux-Arts** Choose from the Flemish Primitives in the Ancient wing or contemporary works in the Modern collection (see page 83).

- **Chocolate** Sweet, sinful and oh so delicious. The museum dedicated to its development is worth sinking your teeth into (see page 67).

- **Toone** Much-loved puppet theatre with outlandishly satirical shows performed by highly detailed marionettes (see page 73).

- **Centre Belge de la Bande Dessinée** In this land of Tintin and Hergé, don't miss this excellent collection of contemporary comic strips (see page 60).

- **Beer, glorious beer** Brussels is the city to go to for the widest selection of beer (see pages 73–5).

⊘ *The fascinating Musée Royaux des Beaux-Arts*

Your brief guide to seeing and experiencing the best of Brussels, depending on the time you have available.

HALF-DAY: BRUSSELS IN A HURRY

Head straight for the Grand Place and explore the guild houses that line this lovely square. From here, join a tour of the historic Hôtel de Ville and then grab some *frites* from one of the nearby vendors.

1 DAY: TIME TO SEE A LITTLE MORE

Begin your visit by taking in the beauty of the Grand Place. Head south out of the square to visit the Manneken Pis – you'll know you're there when you spot the crowds. Have lunch in a local café and then head over to Lower Town to enjoy the shopping opportunities, making sure you don't miss the Galeries St-Hubert arcade with its luxury boutiques.

2–3 DAYS: SHORT CITY-BREAK

Two or three days is the average length of a stay in Brussels, and there is much you can do to make the most of your time. Pack your first day with the suggestions above and then head straight to Upper Town on the morning of your second day. Here is where you will find the best art galleries and museums in the city.

LONGER: ENJOYING BRUSSELS TO THE FULL

To experience all that Brussels has to offer, you need to leave the Petit Ring. Spend a day in Ixelles for colourful African culture and unique boutiques. Visit the EU Quarter to understand the inner workings of the European Parliament, and end your day by watching the sunset from the Atomium.

● *Don't fight the temptation – make the time to indulge*

Something for nothing

On a budget? Never fear. You don't need to break the bank to have a good time in Brussels. Most of the city's finest sights are absolutely free. Even a tasty snack only costs a euro or two if you know where to look.

Grand Place is the heart of the city and a stop to admire the architecture won't even cost you the fluff in your pocket. The guild houses that circle the square showcase the Golden Age of the city when merchants ruled the nation. While each house is unique, they all come together in a satisfying swirl with a heavy Italian baroque influence.

Manneken Pis, the symbol of the city, is also free of charge and just a few steps south of the square on Rue de l'Etuve. It may shock you when you see the famous peeing boy, as the fountain is a lot smaller than you would expect. Gates surround the Manneken Pis to protect him from graffiti and protesters. Luckily he is mounted on a pedestal to give tourists greater viewing opportunities.

Churches are another source of affordable tourist possibilities. The city's places of worship are particularly fascinating due to the number of battles between Catholics and Protestants that were fought during the troubled Reformation and Counter-Reformation period. Some of the more intriguing churches include the four Notre Dames of Bon Secours, de la Chapelle, du Finistère and aux Riches Claires.

The great outdoors is well loved by residents and there are plenty of glorious parks in which to enjoy a day strolling through the shaded lawns. The most interesting is the Parc du

Cinquantenaire. King Léopold II had the park built in order to commemorate the 50th anniversary of the founding of the Belgian nation. These days it is surrounded by a number of cultural institutions allowing visitors to combine a walk in the woods with a bit of inspiring art and architecture.

○ *Brussels has many interesting churches you can visit for free*

When it rains

Upper Town is the place to go when the rain comes tumbling down – and in Brussels you can be pretty sure that this will happen at least once during your visit. The Upper Town neighbourhood is a great location to kill a few hours because of its collection of large museums and galleries, particularly the combined Musée d'Art Ancien and Musée d'Art Moderne connected by a covered walkway.

If these galleries don't take your fancy, there are plenty of other options in the immediate vicinity, including the Palais Royal, Musée des Instruments de Musique, Palais de Charles de Lorraine, Palais de Charles V and Musée de la Dynastie.

With kids in tow, the Musical Instrument Museum is the best of the bunch, as tired tots may get a little sick of wandering through historical room after historical room. Alternatively, take them to the Musée du Cinéma where you can watch a silent film from the early days of cinema complete with piano accompaniment.

Another great option if you want to stick close to the Grand Place is the Scientastic Museum. Children and adults alike love the interactive displays which explore the wonders of science. Factsheets are available in English.

Finally, if you plan ahead, try and book yourself tickets to see the show at the Toone puppet theatre. Eight generations of puppet masters from the same family have built this company into a national treasure. Be warned, performances at the Toone are heavy on satire and only in Flemish. But while many of the jokes will go over your head (unless you happen to be fluent in

Flemish), you'll appreciate the artistry of the puppets and attention to detail.

If all else fails and you're desperate to do some damage to your wallet, head to a *galerie*. There are a few of these covered shopping walkways dotted in and around the Petit Ring, of which the Galeries St-Hubert is the best known. Here is where you will find exclusive boutiques and high-end wares suitable for primo souvenir hunters.

🔺 *Galeries St-Hubert is an excellent place to avoid the weather*

On arrival

TIME DIFFERENCES

Belgian clocks follow Central European Time (CET). During
Daylight Saving Time (end Mar–end Oct), the clocks are put
forward 1 hour. In the Belgian summer, at 12.00 noon, time
elsewhere is as follows.

Australia Eastern Standard Time 20.00, Central Standard Time
19.30, Western Standard Time 18.00
New Zealand 22.00
South Africa 12.00
UK and Republic of Ireland 11.00
US and Canada Newfoundland Time 07.30, Atlantic Canada Time
07.00, Eastern Standard Time 06.00, Central Time 05.00,
Mountain Time 04.00, Pacific Time 03.00, Alaska 02.00

ARRIVING
By air

Most air travellers to Brussels will arrive at Zaventem
International Airport. There are several scheduled airlines that
currently fly into the airport with services from many UK
regional departure points. Charleroi airport is the airport of
choice for Ryanair, located an inconvenient 55 km (34 miles) from
the city centre.

To get to the city centre from Zaventem Airport, take the
Airport City Express train service for the 20-minute journey.
Four departures per hour make the journey between 06.00 and
24.00. Tickets currently cost €2.60 one way. From Charleroi,

either take the Ryanair shuttle bus, which currently costs €10 one way, or board public bus number 68 and connect to the half-hourly train from Charleroi Station to Brussels. The journey time is approximately 1 hour.

Charleroi Airport ☎ 07 125 1211 🅦 www.charleroi-airport.com
Zaventem Airport ☎ 090 070 000 🅦 www.brusselsairport.be
Airport City Express Train ☎ 02 528 2828 🅦 www.b-rail.be
British Airways ☎ 0870 850 9850 🅦 www.ba.com
Ryanair 🅦 www.ryanair.com
SN Brussels Airlines ☎ 0870 735 2345 🅦 www.flysn.co.uk
VLM ☎ 03 230 9000 🅦 www.flyvlm.com

By rail

Eurostar trains from the UK arrive at the Gare du Midi, southwest of the city centre. Check-in for trains on the return journey needs to

● *Gare Centrale is very near the Grand Place*

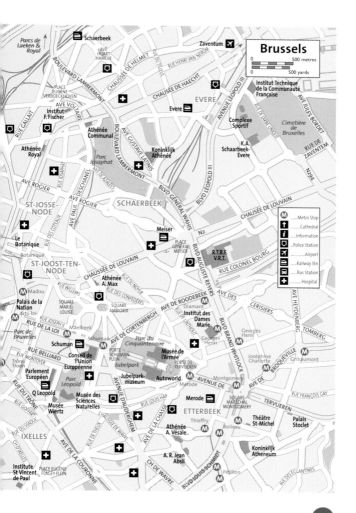

be completed a minimum of 20 minutes before departure. Journey time to and from London Waterloo is approximately 2 hours 20 minutes. From all other points in Europe, trains arrive at the Gare Centrale, slightly east of the city centre.

By road

Belgium is an easy country to drive in. Streets are well marked and well lit, and the motorway system is fast, efficient and extensive. From the coast and ferries bringing visitors from the UK, take the E40/A10 straight to the city via Gent. Alternatively, take the E19 south from the Netherlands, or follow the E314/A2 through the Netherlands from Germany. Once you reach the ring road that circles the city, it is relatively easy to get into the centre by following the motorway signs. Parking is available both on-street and in car parks. Consider selecting a hotel with parking if you plan on bringing your car, as daily rates can add up.

FINDING YOUR FEET

Brussels is a large city of individual neighbourhoods. When exploring specific districts, walking is the best option. For travel between districts, the extensive metro, bus and tram systems are incredibly efficient. Metro trains run regularly and whizz visitors off to almost every corner of the city.

ORIENTATION

Brussels is an extremely easy city to navigate in terms of neighbourhood locations, but difficult once you get to street level. In the city centre, streets are compact, cobbled and wind in all sorts of directions.

One easy way to keep track of your location is to remember that the Centre Monnaie is essentially the main intersection of the Lower Town, while Grand Place and the Gare Centrale act as the bridge into Upper Town, with the Parc aux Bruxelles lying at the heart of the Upper Town district.

A circle of boulevards known as the Petit Ring runs around the city centre, effectively separating it from the outlying districts. Travellers visiting Brussels will most likely base themselves somewhere within the Petit Ring unless they are visiting on business, when a location in the EU Quarter might prove more convenient.

If you travel by Eurostar, you will arrive at the Gare du Midi, to the southwest of the city centre. From the Gare du Midi, it's just a short metro hop to the sights, hotels and cafés of the Lower Town.

GETTING AROUND

An integrated tram, metro and bus system operated by the STIB/MIVB can take you to pretty much every point in the city you might want to visit. Metro trains and trams start running at 05.30 and finish at 24.00. Tickets for all the listed methods of

IF YOU GET LOST, TRY ...

Do you speak English?
Parlez-vous anglais?
Pahrlayvoo ahnglay?

Is this the way to...?
C'est la bonne direction pour...?
Seh lah bon deerekseeawng poor...?

Can you point to it on my map?
Pouvez-vous me le montrer sur la carte?
Poovehvoo mer ler mawngtreh sewr lah kart?

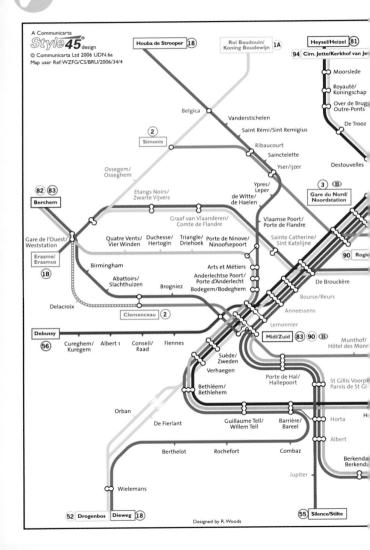

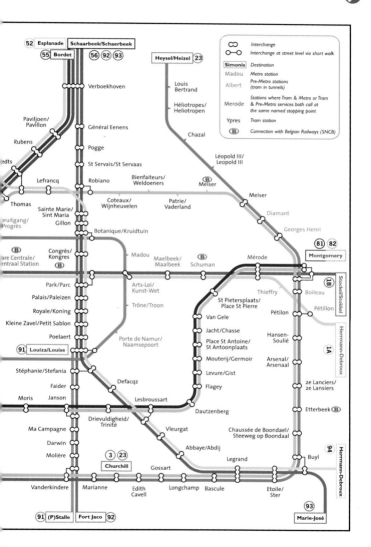

52 Esplanade | Schaarbeek/Schaerbeek

55 Bordet | 56 92 93

Heysel/Heizel 23

Key

∞ Interchange

○—○ Interchange at street level via short walk

Simonis Destination

Madou Metro station

Albert Pre-Metro stations (tram in tunnels)

Merode Stations where Tram & Metro or Tram & Pre-Metro services both call at the same named stopping point

Ypres Tram station

B Connection with Belgian Railways (SNCB)

Verboekhoven

Louis Bertrand

Paviljoen/Pavillon

Général Eenens

Héliotropes/Heliotropen

Rubens

Pogge

Chazal

edts

St Servais/St Servaas

Léopold III/Leopold III

Lefrancq

Robiano

Bienfaiteurs/Weldoeners

B Meiser

Thomas

Sainte Marie/Sint Maria

Meiser

oruitgang/Progrès

Gillon

Coteaux/Wijnheuvelen

Patrie/Vaderland

Diamant

Botanique/Kruidtuin

Georges Henri

B are Centrale/entraal Station B

Congrès/Kongres B

Madou

Maelbeek/Maalbeek

B Schuman

Mérode

81 82

Montgomery

Park/Parc

Arts-Loi/Kunst-Wet

Thieffry

Boileau

B Stockel/Stokkel

Palais/Paleizen

Trône/Troon

St Pietersplaats/Place St Pierre

Pétillon

Pétillon

Royale/Koning

Van Gele

Kleine Zavel/Petit Sablon

Jacht/Chasse

Hansen-Soulié

Hermann-Debroux

1A

Poelaert

Porte de Namur/Naamsepoort

Place St Antoine/St Antoonplaats

91 Louiza/Louise

Mouterij/Germoir

Arsenal/Arsenaal

Stéphanie/Stefania

Levure/Gist

Faider

Defacqz

Flagey

2e Lanciers/2e Lansiers

Moris

Janson

Lesbroussart

Dautzenberg

Etterbeek B

Ma Campagne

Drievuldigheid/Trinité

Vleurgat

Chaussée de Boondael/Steenweg op Boondaal

Darwin

Abbaye/Abdij

94

Buyl

Hermann-Debroux

Molière

3 23

Churchill

Gossart

Legrand

Etoile/Ster

Vanderkindere

Marianne

Edith Cavell

Longchamp

Bascule

93

Marie-José

91 (P)Stalle | Fort Jaco 92

transport can be purchased from metro and rail stations, newsagents, info centres, and on buses and trains. Single tickets valid for a 1-hour journey currently cost from €1.40, while day passes good for unlimited travel are €3.80. Alternatively, purchase a carnet (or 'book') of ten tickets for around €9.80 or a Brussels Card designed for tourists that offers three days of unlimited public transport and admission to 30 museums for €30. Children under six travelling with an adult who has purchased the card can travel free.

STIB/MIVB ⓣ 02 515 2000 ⓦ www.stib.be

CAR HIRE

If you are planning a trip out to Antwerp, Gent or somewhere further afield, you may want to hire a car.
ⓘ Rates vary according to season and length of hire, but special offers are available – check the internet.
ⓘ The minimum age for renting an economy car is 21.

Avis ⓐ Rue Colonel Bourg 107 ⓣ 02 720 0944 ⓦ www.avis.be
ⓛ 08.00–18.00 Mon–Fri ⓜ Metro: Diamant
Budget ⓐ Avenue Louise 327B ⓣ 02 646 5130 ⓦ www.budget.be
ⓛ 08.00–18.00 Mon–Fri, 09.00–12.00 Sat ⓜ Metro: Louise
Hertz ⓐ Boulevard Maurice Lemonnier 8 ⓦ www.hertz.be
ⓛ 07.30–18.00 Mon–Thur, 07.30–19.00 Fri, 08.00–12.00 Sat, 08.00–14.00 Sun ⓜ Metro: Anneessens

ⓓ *The clock at Mont des Arts*

Lower Town

When you think of Belgium, the sights you most associate with the
country can all be found in the winding streets of Brussels' Lower
Town. Here is where the Manneken Pis piddles away to the delight
of his thousands of daily admirers, where the grace and elegance
of the Grand Place seduces fans of architecture, and where
boutiques peek out from walls of ancient buildings enticing
visitors with their displays of lace and mouthwatering chocolate.

Also included in Lower Town's 'borders' are the historical
heart of the district, St-Géry, which is where the first buildings
of the city were constructed centuries ago, and the ancient port
area of Ste-Catherine, now known for its seafood restaurants.

Finally, in the southeast corner of Lower Town is Les Marolles,
a working-class district with a strong sense of community that
battles every day against encroaching gentrification.

SIGHTS & ATTRACTIONS

Centre Belge de la Bande Dessinée

Belgians love humour and art. So it should come as no surprise
that there is a museum dedicated to the art of the comic strip.
While the work of Hergé and the story of Tintin make up a large
section of the collection, there's plenty more than just images of
Snowy to stare at.
❶ Be warned: this museum is a cerebral examination of the
comic and not designed with kids in mind. ⓐ Rue des Sables 20
❶ 02 219 1980 ⓦ www.brusselsbdtour.com ❶ 10.00–18.00
Tues–Sun ⓝ Metro: Rogier. Admission charge

Grand Place & Hôtel de Ville

Once described by Victor Hugo as the most beautiful square in the world, the Grand Place is the spiritual heart of the city. Now given UNESCO World Heritage Site status, it is the most visited spot in Brussels – and for good reason.

The Grand Place developed its distinctive look thanks to the influential city guilds. The guilds craved power. In order to achieve this, they needed two things: a strong base and proximity to City Hall. As each guild grew in prominence, they built or branded homes close to City Hall and added markings to signify their status. Therefore, a statue of the patron saint of tallow dealers exists outside their former guild house, while the

⬤ *Numerous ornate fountains embellish the Grand Place*

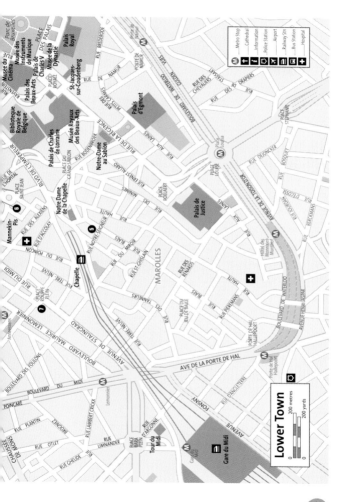

LOWER TOWN

63

detail of a hop plant is carved above the door to the brewers' guild. Some of the more noteworthy guild houses include the haberdashers' guild house, the brewers' guild house and the artists' guild.

What makes Grand Place so special is the architecture. The plots of land that the houses lie on are extremely small, giving grace and elegance to the compact yet ornate Italian baroque style. The crowning glory is the Hôtel de Ville (City Hall) built in the early 15th century. This amazing building took 50 years to build with ornate wings, a belfry and a 113 m (371 ft) tower with a gilded statue of St Michael slaying the dragon at the very top. You'll note that the left wing may seem smaller than the right. This is not a mistake. Rather, it was a conscious decision made in order to accommodate the existing street grid pattern. A guided tour taking visitors through the beautiful official rooms is highly recommended. However, visitors are not permitted in the tower.

Hôtel de Ville ⓐ Grand Place ⓣ 02 279 4365. ⓛ Guided tours in English 15.15 Tues–Wed, Apr–Sept, 10.45 & 12.15 Sun (year-round) ⓝ Metro: Bourse

Manneken Pis

Belgium's national symbol is actually a lot smaller than you might think. Always surrounded by crowds, the fountain is now blocked off by gated railings to protect him from admirers. On special days, he is costumed to reflect the season. Look for the nearby framed sign to see when he is next set to don a colourful outfit. Try to go early in the day or late in the afternoon for the best view.

ⓐ Rue de l'Etuve ⓝ Metro: Bourse

Notre-Dame de Bon-Secours

For an example of Flemish Renaissance architecture, look no further than this baroque church built in the late 1600s – widely considered to be the most beautiful in the district.

ⓐ Rue du Marché au Charbon ① 02 514 3113 ① 09.00–17.00 winter; 09.00–18.00 summer Ⓝ Metro: Anneessens

Notre-Dame de la Chapelle

This is the ultimate mish-mash of a building. The original chapel was built in the 12th century; the nave is 15th-century Gothic; and the art collection is largely 19th century. It is the burial place of civil rights campaigner Francois Annessens and of Pieter Brueghel the Elder and his wife.

ⓐ Place de la Chapelle ① 02 512 0737 ① 09.00–16.00 June–Sept; 12.00–16.00 Oct–May Ⓝ Metro: Anneessens

Notre-Dame du Finistère

Once the site of a 15th-century chapel, the present church was built on top of the existing structure in the early 18th century. The most noteworthy feature is the wildly baroque pulpit.

ⓐ Rue Neuve ① 02 217 5252 ① 08.00–18.00 Mon–Sat, 08.00–12.00, 15.00–18.00 Sun Ⓝ Metro: De Brouckère

Notre-Dame aux Riches Claires

It is believed that this church was designed and built in 1665 by a student of Rubens named Luc Fayd'herbe. Renovations re-energised the structure in 2000.

ⓐ Rue des Riches Claires 23 ① 02 511 0937 ① 16.00–18.00 Sat, 09.30–14.00 Sun Ⓝ Metro: Bourse

Ste-Catherine

This church has experienced a wealth of history and has a number of unsavoury features including a purpose-built pissoir (public urinal) constructed in between its buttresses. Unloved by the local populace, it was almost transformed into the city stock exchange before opening its doors to its congregation in 1867. Today, it is a graceful house of worship filled with stained-glass windows and minor art treasures.

Place Ste-Catherine ❶ 02 513 3481 ❷ 08.30–17.00 Mon–Sat, 09.00–12.00 Sun

St-Jean-Baptiste au Béguinage

Another example of Flemish baroque architecture, this church features a warm amber-hued façade and a collection of 17th-century paintings by Theodoor van Loon.

Place du Béguinage ❶ 02 217 8742 ❷ 09.00–17.00 Metro: Ste-Catherine

St-Nicholas

This elegant church was founded in the 11th century and features a moody Gothic interior that is set to be unveiled later this year following an extensive renovation. The curves of the walls follow the old course of the River Senne.

Rue au Beurre 1 ❶ 02 513 8 022 ❷ Check for details; at the time of going to print the church was undergoing restoration Metro: Bourse

CULTURE

Musée des Brasseurs Belges

This museum has a permanent collection that examines both ancient and modern methods of brewing beer.

ⓐ Grand Place 10 ❶ 02 511 4987 ⓦ www.biere2005.be/informations/wallonia_attraction/FR/C/V/15792.html
❶ 10.00–17.00 daily (summer); 10.00–16.30 Mon–Fri, 12.00–16.30 Sat & Sun (winter) Ⓝ Metro: Bourse. Admission charge

Musée du Cacao et du Chocolat

Chocolate was introduced to the world by the Aztecs and this museum examines the journey the sweet stuff has taken since that time. Seminal moments include the development of praline and the history of the industry in Belgium.

ⓐ Rue de la Tête d'Or 9/11 ❶ 02 514 2048 ⓦ www.mucc.be
❶ 10.00–17.00 daily (summer); 10.00–17.00 Tues–Sun (winter)
Ⓝ Metro: Bourse. Admission charge

Musée de la Ville de Bruxelles

When this building was constructed in the 13th century it was known as the Broodhuis (or 'bread house'), as it was owned by the bakers' guild. Today it holds the museum of the city of Brussels. Collections include some rather faded tapestries, but it's the wardrobe of more than 600 costumes designed for the Manneken Pis and some delightful Breughel paintings that really draw the crowds.

ⓐ Grand Place ❶ 02 279 4350 ⓦ www.brucity.be ❶ 10.00–17.00 Tues–Sun Ⓝ Metro: Bourse. Admission charge

RETAIL THERAPY

Shopping streets & markets

In Lower Town, the streets around Grand Place and the Manneken Pis are chock full of Belgian tourist tat, including cut-rate chocolatiers, 'Made in China' lace shops and boutiques celebrating the EU government. For something a little more authentic, go instead to the Rue des Eperonniers southeast of the square.

Glamour can be added to your life in the form of the shops of the Galeries St-Hubert, a famous shopping arcade opened in 1847 that is home to a collection of boutiques selling handmade and well-crafted clothing, accessories, hats and lace.

High-street labels can be found on the Rue Neuve – the Oxford Street or Fifth Avenue of Brussels. Here is where you will come across well-known European labels such as Benetton, Zara and H&M. The northern end of the street also boasts City 2, a large shopping centre, and a branch of the Inno department store. If the crowds start to niggle at your nerves, get off the street and head instead to the unique boutiques and independent shops of the Rue des Fripiers or Rue du Marché aux Herbes.

Better yet, if unique and independent really are what you prefer when you're digging out your wallet, head down to the neighbourhoods of Ste-Catherine and St-Géry. The Rue Antoine Dansaert is shopping central for street wear, quirky gifts, and cutting-edge design and furnishings. Young designers often make this their first stop when looking for locations to build their first boutique.

Vieux Marché

One person's junk is another's treasure at this flea market located in a vibrant immigrant neighbourhood. If you lack the patience to rummage through everything on display, go instead to the antique shops that line Rue Blaes and Rue Haute. Be aware of your wallets and purses if you do decide to visit, as the Les Marolles district (where the market is situated) has a reputation for petty theft. ⓐ Place du Jeu de Balle Ⓜ Metro: Porte de Hal

TAKING A BREAK

Chéz Leon £ ❶ If you have the kids in tow but want to try some cracking Belgian cuisine, then this buzzy restaurant should fit the bill. The paper napkins and photographed menus give the place a fast-food feel, but that shouldn't dissuade you from trying the delicious local favourites such as *moules frites* (mussels and chips). Children under 12 get a free set menu when accompanied by two paying adults – a godsend for parents of fussy eaters. ⓐ Rue des Bouchers 18 Ⓣ 02 511 1415 Ⓦ www.chezleon.be Ⓛ 12.00–23.00 Mon–Thur & Sun, 12.00–23.30 Fri & Sat Ⓜ Metro: Bourse

Bij den Boer ££ ❷ It ain't pretty, but this greasy-spoon style establishment dishes up stunning pots of mussels and thick, rich bouillabaisse. Service is horrible – and there is no point complaining – but you won't be rushed when you finally do get your food. A great place for a lazy winter afternoon. ⓐ Quai aux Briques 60 Ⓣ 02 512 6122 Ⓦ www.bijdenboer.com Ⓛ 12.00–14.30, 18.00–22.30 Mon–Sat Ⓜ Metro: Ste-Catherine

AFTER DARK

Restaurants

In 't Spinnekopke £–££ ❸ Housed in a pretty cottage-style building, this cosy restaurant masters the art of dishing up hearty Belgian stews and fish dishes. Perfect for a rainy day when you need a bit of warmth in your belly and a beer to wash it down with. Service can be hit and miss. ❷ Place du Jardin aux Fleurs 1 ❶ 02 511 8695 ❸ 12.00–15.00, 18.00–23.00 Mon–Thur, 12.00–15.00, 18.00–24.00 Fri, 18.00–24.00 Sat ❻ Metro: Bourse

⬥ La Roue d'Or is a great place to try local cuisine

Belga Queen ££ ❹ All Belgian – all the time. That's what this restaurant is famous for. From the interiors to the food to the hinges on the doors – everything is made in Belgium and all the fresher for it. Once a bank, its large ceilings and imposing look make it more of a place for groups than romancing couples.
ⓐ Rue du Fossé aux Loups 32 ❶ 02 217 2187
🕑 12.00–14.30, 19.00–24.00 Ⓝ Metro: De Brouckère

L'Idiot du Village ££–£££ ❺ The hip and happening of the city have fallen in love with this bohemian establishment featuring eclectic food and interiors. You will too. ⓐ Rue Notre-Seigneur 19
❶ 02 502 5582 🕑 12.00–14.00, 19.30–23.00 Mon–Fri Ⓝ Buses: 27, 48, 95, 96

La Roue d'Or ££–£££ ❻ If you have any desire to try Belgian food, then this is the place to do it. Mussels, oysters, rabbit, pig's trotter, lamb's tongue – it's all here. Much more delicious than it sounds. An English menu is available if you get into trouble.
ⓐ Rue des Chapeliers 26 ⓐ 02 514 2554
🕑 12.00–24.00 Ⓝ Metro: Bourse

Comme Chez Soi £££ ❼ Considered by many to be the best restaurant in the country, this intimate eatery features fine art nouveau interiors and inventive, yet flavourful, menus. The house speciality of fillet of sole with white mousseline and shrimp is never dropped from the always-changing bill of fare. Ardent non-smokers should be warned that ventilation is poor.
ⓐ Place Rouppe 23 ❶ 02 512 2921 🕑 12.00–14.15, 19.00–23.00 Tues–Sat Ⓝ Metro: Anneessens

Bars, clubs & discos

The Fuse More than 2,000 clubbers pack into this superclub which is heavy on international DJs and light on upkept interiors. Expect deep house and up-for-it crowds. Rue Blaes 208 02 511 9789 www.fuse.be 22.00–05.00 Thur, 22.00–07.00 Fri & Sat Metro: Porte de Hal

Recyclart New talent is the mainstay of this electronic venue. Built as part of an urban regeneration project, it features tomorrow's big names today. When it's good, it's really, really good. But when it's bad, it's awful. Go with no expectations and you'll be likely to have the best night of your stay. Gare de Bruxelles-Chapelle, Rue des Ursulines 02 502 5734 www.recyclart.be Opening times vary Metro: Gare Centrale

Ric's Boat Float while you flail at this kicking hardcore venue located in a boat moored on a Brussels canal. The monthly NEMO party is legendary for fans of deep underground tunes. Quai des Peniches 44B 02 203 6728 Opening times vary Metro: Yser

Le Soixante replaced the very successful Pablo Discobar. If you like Techno, Electrohouse and Drum & Bass, you should visit. Its atmoshere is bright and friendly, its doors open free of charge. Rue du Marché aux Charbon 02 514 5149 www.soixante.be Wed–Sun Metro: Bourse

Cinemas & theatres

Théâtre National This national theatre caters for the French-speaking community of Belgium. Programming includes everything from new works by local playwrights to old classics produced with a contemporary edge. ⓐ Boulevard Anspach 85 ⓣ 02 203 5303 ⓦ www.theatrenational.be ⓑ Box office: 10.00–18.00 Mon–Fri ⓜ Metro: Bourse

Toone The Toone puppet theatre has passed through the same family for eight generations and continues to produce riotous puppet shows to sell-out crowds. There are now more than 1,300 puppets with new ones being prepared every year as public figures gain prominence. ⓐ Petite Rue des Bouchers 21 ⓣ 02 217 2753 ⓑ Hours and performance times vary ⓜ Metro: Bourse

KNOWING YOUR BEER

When it comes to beer, the bottles brewed in Belgium are considered by most to be the finest in the world. There is a brew to suit every occasion, taste and meal – and locals are extremely choosy when selecting their drink of choice. While beer owes its origins to the Middle East more than 10,000 years ago, it was the Romans who popularised the drink in western Europe around the 5th century. Monks had a monopoly on brewing and used the profits to maintain their brewing facilities.

When the Middle Ages arrived, the guilds took control of the industry and the number of breweries increased hugely. By the 16th century, beer and ale were staples of society and profits were huge.

At its peak in 1900, there were more than 3,000 breweries in the country. Unfortunately, two world wars, the Great Depression and the popularisation of the cocktail culture have reduced that number to about 100. Does this mean that beer-making in Belgium is over? On the contrary, it has ensured that only the finest breweries have survived and drinking the golden-hued liquid is more popular than ever.

While there are few breweries in Brussels, the city is the best place to plan a beer-tasting tour as the bars offer the widest selection of bottles from the most breweries. The beer museum on Grand Place is a good place to go for a brief overview of the industry, with a day trip to Leuven an absolute must if you want to challenge your taste buds further.

When embarking on a tasting session at a Belgian bar, you'll find that a typical establishment will usually have on tap a draught lager such as Stella Artois or Maes and a wheat beer such as Hoegaarden. Wheat beer is generally considered to be more of a summer drink and is usually served in large tankards. A better bar will expand on this selection with offerings from more obscure breweries.

The Holy Grail of beers are the Trappist varieties produced by Trappist monks in the towns of Chimay, Westmalle, Orval, Rochefort and Westvleteren. These beers are for the pros and pack a killer alcoholic kick. A standard variety will be dark brown and creamy. However, there are double and triple versions that are even stronger, darker and creamier.

Other unique brews are Lambics (which are naturally fermented without the use of yeast and often developed in the Brussels area), Gueuze (which mixes older and younger versions of Lambic for an acquired taste) and fruit beers (which range from ultra tart to sweet).

If you're looking to bring a few bottles of your favourite find back home, it is possible to arrange shipping. Alternatively, stock up at any supermarket.

Musée des Brasseurs Belges ⓐ Grand Place ⓣ 02 511 4987 ⓦ www.biere2005.be/informations/wallonia_attraction/ FR/C/V/15792.html ⓛ 10.00–17.00 daily (summer); 10.00–16.30 Mon–Fri, 12.00–16.30 Sat & Sun (winter) ⓝ Metro: Bourse. Admission charge

⬤ *The agonizing dilemma of having to choose*

Upper Town

Situated on the top of a hill, Brussels' Upper Town was created on the orders of King Lambert II in order to move the royal family away from the murky and smelly waters of the River Senne. Nobles and wealthy merchants followed and transformed the area into the neighbourhood that can be seen today – a collection of palaces, parks, museums and government buildings ripe for exploration. But if that doesn't entice, the elegant shopping and supping in Sablon should. An evening in this elegant square will make you feel like a king.

SIGHTS & ATTRACTIONS

Cathédrale des Sts Michel et Gudule

Since its completion, this church dedicated to the male and female patron saints of the city has survived graffiti attacks by Protestants and looting by French Revolutionary forces. Today it is a symbol of the city due to its glorious stained-glass windows and 11th-century Romanesque crypt.

ⓐ Place Ste Gudule ⓣ 02 217 8345 ⓦ www.cathedralestmichel.be ⓛ 08.00–18.00 ⓜ Metro: Gare Centrale. Admission charge

Notre-Dame au Sablon

Having emerged from a recent renovation, this church was built to accommodate a statue of Mary shipped in from Antwerp which allegedly had healing powers. Unfortunately the statue was destroyed by Protestants during the iconoclastic riots. The statue's arrival continues to be celebrated every July during

Ommegang celebrations. See page 14 for details on this citywide festival.

ⓐ Rue de la Régence 3B ⓣ 02 511 5741 ⓛ 09.00–19.00 Mon–Sat
Ⓝ Metro: Porte de Namur

🔺 *The exquisite detailing of Notre-Dame au Sablon*

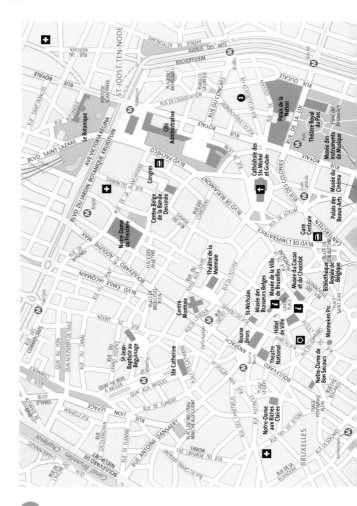

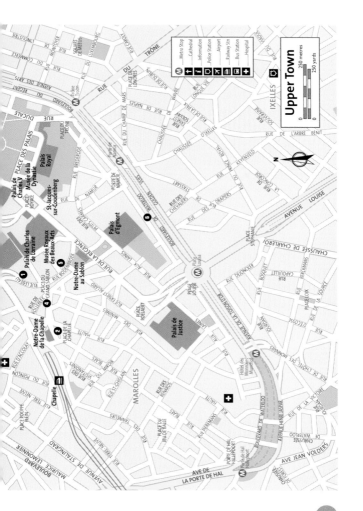

Upper Town

Metro Stop
Cathedral
Information
Police Station
Airport
Railway Stn
Bus Station
Hospital

0   250 metres
0   250 yards

Palais de Charles de Lorraine

Opened in 2000, this museum looks at the lifestyles of the rich and famous during the 18th century. Focus is placed on the achievements of Charles of Lorraine, the governor-general of the Austrian-Netherlands.

ⓐ Place du Musée 1 ⓣ 02 519 5807 ⓦ www.kbr.be ⓛ 13.00–17.00 Tues–Fri, 10.00–17.00 Sat, 10.00–17.00 first Sun of the month ⓝ Metro: Gare Centrale. Admission charge

Palais de Charles V

Step back in time by exploring the excavated remains of the former palace of Belgium's nobility. Destroyed by a devastating fire in 1731, the palace was never rebuilt – but recent archaeological work has uncovered the remains of some of the rooms. The streets surrounding the remains date back to the same period and are just as fascinating as the site itself.

ⓐ Place des Palais 7 ⓣ 02 545 0800 ⓛ 10.00–18.00 Tues–Sun, June–Sept; 10.00–17.00 Tues–Sun, Oct–May. Admission charge.

Palais de Justice

More than 3,000 houses were razed to build this massive palace for Léopold II, which drove the architect mad during the course of the project's completion. No one can quite agree what style the palace was built in, but the symmetry is perfect and incredibly imposing. If you have to choose one palace to visit, make this the one.

ⓐ Place Poelaert ⓣ 02 508 6410 ⓛ 08.00–17.00 Mon–Fri ⓝ Metro: Louise

Palais Royal

This residential palace lacks the charm of some of the other stately homes of the city and features a mish-mash of architectural styles due to a near-constant policy of remodelling begun in 1825.

ⓐ Place des Palais ❶ 02 551 2 020 ⓦ www.monarchie.be
🕓 Hours vary, Tues–Sun from late July–late Sept Ⓜ Metro: Trône

Place Royale

Built on the ruins of the palace of the Dukes of Brabant, this elegant square possesses beautiful examples of neoclassical architecture in the heart of the city's Upper Town. Grand Place and the Lower Town may have been the focus of power during the 17th and 18th centuries, but the Austrian overlords moved government to this locale during their period of rule. Restoration of the buildings is ongoing, so don't be surprised if some of the façades are covered with scaffolding.

Ⓜ Trams: 92, 93, 94

St-Jacques-sur-Coudenberg

Built to look like a Roman temple in 1775, this church possesses an ancient resemblance that was slightly ruined by the addition of a bell tower in the 19th century. Despite this anomaly, the building remains quite imposing with an exterior and interior intended to create fear and awe in the minds of visiting worshippers.

ⓐ Impasse Borgendael 1 ❶ 02 511 7836 🕓 10.00–17.45
Ⓜ Metro: Trône

CULTURE

Musée du Cinéma

Film buffs will love this museum, which looks at the dawn of film and early cinematography. It is still possible to catch a silent film in the working cinema .

ⓐ Palais des Beaux-Arts, Rue Baron Horta 9 ⓣ 02 507 8370
ⓦ www.cinematheque.be ⓛ 17.30–22.30 ⓜ Metro: Gare Centrale.
Admission charge

Musée de la Dynastie

Examine the history of the Belgian royal family at this museum chronicling the life and times of the illustrious clan. Of particular interest is an extensive collection of items once owned and used by King Baudouin I.

ⓐ Place des Palais 7 ⓣ 02 511 5578 ⓦ www.musbellevue.be
ⓛ 10.00–16.00 Tues–Sun ⓜ Metro: Gare Centrale. Admission charge

Musée des Instruments de Musique

Housed in a former department store, it took over a decade of restoration to create this museum dedicated to musical instruments. The collection boasts more than 6,000 items, of which 1,500 are on revolving display. As Belgium is the home of the creator of the saxophone, it should come as no surprise that there is an extensive section examining the development of the instrument, including a number of bizarre prototypes.

ⓐ Rue Montagne de la Cour 2 ⓣ 02 545 0130
ⓦ www.mim.fgov.be ⓛ 09.30–17.00 Tues–Fri, 10.00–17.00 Sat & Sun ⓜ Metro: Gare Centrale

Musée Royaux des Beaux-Arts

The Musée Royaux des Beaux-Arts (Royal Fine Arts Museum) is one of the finest in Belgium. The collection is divided into two branches, each devoted to different periods: Modern and Ancient. A covered walkway joins the two, meaning that a single admission fee will get you into both museums. However, you may want to break it up a bit as the place is vast. The collection is particularly strong on painters and artists originating from the Low Countries.

⬤ *Take your time at the Musée des Beaux-Arts*

Musée d'Art Ancien

Flemish painters of the 15th century – the so-called 'Flemish Primitives' – revolutionised the art world with their innovative use of oils. This extensive museum holds many of the finest works from the period, including paintings by Hieronymous Bosch and Memling. Go up a floor for the true masterpieces. Here is where you will find stunning works by favourite sons Rubens, Van Dyck, Jordaans, Breughel the Younger and, particularly, Breughel the Elder. For more modern work, take the underground passage that connects with the Musée d'Art Moderne just next door.
ⓐ Rue de la Régence 3 ⓣ 02 508 32 11 ⓦ www.fine-arts-museum.be ⓛ 10.00–17.00 Tues–Sun. Admission charge

Musée d'Art Moderne

The main entrance to this modern collection of primarily French and Belgian artists is through the house where the writer Alexandre Dumas once lived. The collection showcases works dating from the turn of the 20th century to the present day with a strong focus on Expressionism and Surrealism. Paul Delvaux and René Magritte are well represented. English-language brochures and tours are available.
ⓐ Place Royale 1 ⓣ 02 508 32 11 ⓦ www.fine-arts-museum.be
ⓛ 10.00–17.00 Tues–Sun. Admission charge

RETAIL THERAPY

Place du Grand Sablon The shopping and supping locale choice for the city's elite. A couple of hours spent patrolling through the boutiques and cafés that line the square and surrounding streets is sure to dent your wallet. During weekend mornings, the upper end of the square is transformed into an antiques market. Definitely not for those on a budget. ⓐ Place du Grand Sablon ⓝ Trams: 92, 93, 94

TAKING A BREAK

Le Cap Sablon £–££ ❶ Rest your weary feet at this comfortable brasserie with typical Belgian dishes livened up with unexpected spices. There is a terrace that is popular during the summer months, but you'll need to book a table and specify the section when making your reservation. ⓐ Rue Lebeau 75 ⓣ 02 512 0170 ⓛ 12.00–23.30 Mon–Wed, 12.00–24.00 Thur–Sun ⓝ Metro: Gare Centrale

AFTER DARK

Restaurants
Aux Marches de la Chapelle £–££ ❷ For something simple and filling, head over to this Belgian eatery strong on brasserie-style dishes such as sauerkraut and dumplings. Not for those on a diet or vegetarians. ⓐ Place de la Chapelle 5 ⓣ 02 512 6891 ⓛ 12.00–15.00, 18.30–23.00 Mon–Fri, 18.30–23.00 Sat

Le Poulbot de Bruxelles ££ ❸ This French restaurant caters for the political crowds that come for the tasty, well-prepared dishes and informal atmosphere. Luckily, the fact that the bulk of the clientele work at the parliament buildings doesn't take anything away from the relaxed dining and presentation.

Rue de la Croix de Fer 29 02 513 3861 12.00–14.00, 19.00–22.00 Mon, Wed–Fri, 12.00–14.00 Tues, 19.00–22.00 Sat Metro: Parc

La Clef des Champs ££–£££ Provençal speciality restaurant that looks like it belongs on a street in France. Expect typical dishes from the region. Rue de Rollebeek 23 02 512 1193 12.00–14.30, 18.30–23.00 Tues–Sat Trams: 92, 93, 94

Castello Banfi £££ Probably the best Italian restaurant in town, this chic dining spot serves up mouthwateringly good fare. The mascarpone is to die for. A jacket and tie are a must. Rue Bodenbroek 12 02 512 8794 12.00–14.30, 19.00–22.30 Tues–Sat, 12.00–14.30 Sun, closed last 3 wks in Aug Trams: 92, 93, 94

Maison du Boeuf £££ There's plenty to choose from at this ritzy restaurant, but it's the beef that you should make a beeline for. The house speciality is rib steak roasted in salt – and you should order it if you have the appetite. Gentlemen should note that a jacket and tie are required. Hilton Hotel, Boulevard de Waterloo 38 02 504 1334 12.00–14.30, 19.00–22.30 Metro: Louise

Bars, clubs & discos

Le Bier Circus It ain't much to look at, but this bar is packed full of beer varieties. You might be a bit overwhelmed by the 17 page menu, but the knowledgeable bar staff will help you make an informed selection. Rue de l'Enseignement 89 02 218 0034 www.biercircus.be 12.00–14.30, 18.00–24.00 Mon–Fri Trams: 92, 93, 94

Le Grain de Sable Customers flock to this cocktail-chic establishment due to its jazzy vibe which beckons and large, attractive streetside terrace. The clientele tends to be of the new money, upmarket brigade – but it's a nice place to enjoy a drink nonetheless. ⓐ Place du Grand Sablon 15 ① 02 514 0583 ⓛ 08.00–late Ⓝ Trams: 92, 93, 94

Le Perroquet In summer months, this jewel of an art nouveau establishment is packed with the young, rich and fabulous of the city. However, as the grey months roll in so do the Eurocrats – and the atmosphere turns a tad dour. Go before the after-work rush if you want to bag a seat. ⓐ Rue Watteau 31 ① 02 512 9922 ⓛ 10.00–01.00 Ⓝ Trams: 92, 93, 94

Cinemas & theatres

Théâtre du Rideau de Bruxelles This French-language theatre company is a good place to go if you're looking for safe, reliable productions of historical dramas and modern classics. ⓐ Palais des Beaux-Arts, Rue Ravenstein 23 ① 02 507 8361 ⓦ www.rideaudebruxelles.be ⓛ Box office: 11.00–19.00 Mon–Sat Ⓝ Metro: Gare Centrale

Théâtre Royal du Parc This playhouse, built in 1782, is a real gem. While the productions aren't necessarily at the forefront of theatrical innovation, the interiors should be more than enough to convince you to buy a ticket.
ⓐ Rue de la Loi 3 ① 02 505 3030 ⓦ www.theatreduparc.be
ⓛ Box office: 11.00–18.00 Mon–Fri, 11.00–13.00, 14.00–18.00 Sat, Sun Ⓝ Metro: Arts-Loi or Parc

Beyond the Petit Ring

The neighbourhoods outside the Petit Ring (the ring of boulevards surrounding the Upper and Lower Town) differ greatly in flavour and form. The EU district is tailor-made for government Eurocrats, while Ixelles is packed with colour and excitement due to a vibrant African community. Visitors should be sure to venture beyond the Petit Ring circle.

SIGHTS & ATTRACTIONS

Atomium

This symbol of the city was built as part of the World's Fair celebrations of 1958. A recent renovation has completely

⬤ *View Brussels from the windows of the Atomium*

transformed the once tired exhibits and the structure is once again a sight worth going to. The trip to the top is a 'must do' Brussels experience for most visitors and is well worth the admission charge.

ⓐ Boulevard du Centenaire ⓣ 02 475 4777 ⓦ www.atomium.be ⓛ 09.00–19.00 Apr–Aug; 10.00–17.30 Sept–Mar ⓝ Metro: Heysel. Admission charge

Bois de la Cambre

This vast park is the largest green space in the city. Located on the edge of the city centre, it was originally a section of a much larger forest that was reshaped to allow an avenue to be built through it for access to the countryside.

ⓐ Bois de la Cambre

Collégiale des Sts Pierre et Guidon

The site of this church is one of the oldest in the city, dating back to the 10th century. The current structure was built in the 15th century in the Gothic style and is known for its Romanesque crypts.

ⓐ Place de la Valliance ⓣ 02 523 0220 ⓛ 09.00–12.00, 14.00–17.00 ⓝ Metro: St-Guidon

Ixelles

At its peak, Belgium had large interests in the Congo and Equatorial Africa. While the country's legacy as a colonial nation is murky, Brussels benefited from an influx of citizens from the region. Ixelles is the neighbourhood where most reside in a colourful conglomeration of markets, restaurants and ethnic

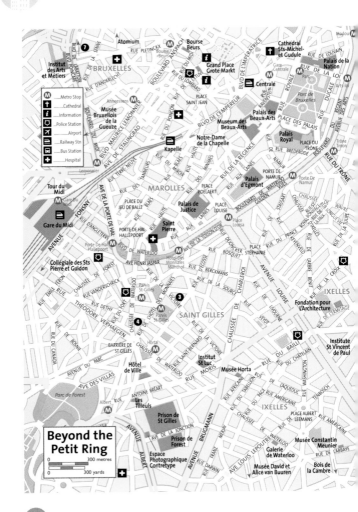

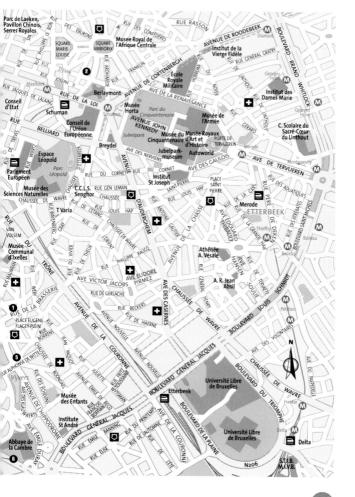

shops. Asian and North Africans also call the area home, making this the district to head to if you want a break from Flemish and French.

 The neighbourhood's centre is located at the corner of Rue Longue Vie and Rue de la Paix

Notre-Dame de Laeken

This massive church is a salute to the Gothic style and was completed in the mid-19th century. The cemetery holds tombs of important locals and a cast of Rodin's *The Thinker*.

 Parvis Notre Dame 02 478 2095 14.00–17.00 Tues–Sun Metro: Bockstael

Parc du Cinquantenaire

This massive park is one of the green lungs of the city and home to some of its finest museums. King Léopold II had the park built by shipping in more than 300 labourers to work around the clock to create the neoclassical structure that calls the park home. The most famous structure inside the park is the Arc de Triomphe, a celebratory arch set for completion in 1880 to commemorate the 50th anniversary of the founding of the Belgian nation. Unfortunately the deadline was missed by about 30 years. Also of note is the Pavilion Horta in the northwest section of the park, which holds a collection of reliefs by the artist Jef Lambeaux.

 Parq du Cinquantenaire Metro: Schuman

Pavillon Chinois

This pavilion was originally built as a restaurant for the royal family and now holds a collection of fine Chinese porcelain.

ⓐ Rue Jules van Praet 44 ⓣ 02 268 1608
ⓦ www.kmkg-mrah.be ⓛ 09.30–17.00 Tues–Fri, 10.00–17.00 Sat
& Sun ⓝ Trams: 23, 52. Admission charge

Serres Royales

Eleven linked greenhouses were commissioned by Léopold II and
designed by a young Horta in the 1870s. A favourite with the
royal family, many members have set up offices and audience
areas within the leafy confines. Normally closed to the public,
the greenhouses open to the hoi polloi for a single month
every May.

ⓐ Avenue du Parc Royal 61 ⓣ 02 513 8940 ⓛ hours vary each
May; check in advance for schedules ⓝ Metro: Heysel.
Admission charge

⬤ You'll find more art collections at the Pavilion Horta

Tour Japonaise

Temporary Japanese exhibitions are held in the faux pagoda surrounded by elegant Japanese gardens.

🅐 Avenue Jules van Praet 44 📞 02 268 1608
🔵 www.kmkg-mrah.be 🕐 09.30–17.00 Tues–Fri, 10.00–17.00 Sat & Sun 🚈 Trams: 23, 52. Admission charge

CULTURE

Autoworld

This comprehensive auto museum chronicles the history of the automobile from 1886 to today.

🅐 Parc du Cinquantenaire 11 📞 02 736 4165
🔵 www.autoworld.be 🕐 10.00–18.00 Apr–Oct; 10.00–17.00 Nov–Mar 🚈 Metro: Mérode. Admission charge

Espace Photographique Contretype

Houses a collection of photography and sponsors artist-in-residence programmes with regular showcases of their work.

🅐 Avenue de la Jonction 1 📞 02 538 4220 🔵 www.contretype.org
🕐 11.00–18.00 Wed–Fri, 13.00–18.00 Sat & Sun 🚈 Trams: 81, 90, 92; Bus: 54. Admission charge

Fondation pour l'Architecture

Tells the story of Brussels' architectural treasures.

🅐 Rue de l'Ermitage 55 📞 02 642 2480
🔵 www.fondationpourlarchitecture.be 🕐 12.00–18.00 Tues & Thur–Sun, 12.00–19.00 Wed 🚈 Trams: 81, 82, 93, 94; Buses: 38, 54, 60. Admission charge

Musée des Sciences Naturelles

Belgium's Royal Natural History Museum boasts a great collection of iguanodons and a stunning new room dedicated to the Arctic and Antarctic environments.

ⓐ Rue Vautier 25 ⓣ 02 627 4238 ⓦ www.naturasciences.be
ⓛ 09.30–16.45 Tues–Fri, 10.00–18.00 Sat & Sun ⓜ Metro: Trône. Admission charge

◆ *Espace Photographique Countretype houses photographic art*

Musée Bruxellois de la Gueuze

This museum is made for beer fans as it takes visitors on a tasting tour around the final brewery that produces Gueuze – an intriguing beer that undergoes a fermenting process unique to the area.

ⓐ Rue Gheude 56 ⓣ 02 521 4928 ⓦ www.cantillon.be
ⓛ 09.00–17.00 Mon–Fri, 10.00–17.00 Sat ⓝ Metro: Clemenceau

Musée Communal d'Ixelles

This enjoyable museum has a choice selection of modern art from the likes of Magritte, Delveaux and Toulouse-Lautrec. The exhibition spaces are small but perfectly formed.

ⓐ Rue Van Volsem 71 ⓣ 02 515 6421 ⓦ www.musee-ixelles.be
ⓛ 13.00–18.30 Tues–Fri, 10.00–17.00 Sat & Sun ⓝ Buses: 38, 54, 60, 71. Admission charge

Musée David et Alice van Buuren

Art deco is celebrated at this home of a wealthy collector addicted to the movement. The clean lines of the architecture act as a beautiful backdrop to the art collection, which includes works by Breughel and Van Gogh.

ⓐ Avenue Léo Errera 41 ⓣ 02 343 4851
ⓦ www.museumvanbuuren.com ⓛ 13.00–18.00 Sun & Mon, 14.00–18.00 Wed ⓝ Trams: 23, 90; Buses: 38, 60. Admission charge

Musée d'Erasmus

Dutch humanist and theologian Erasmus stayed in this home whenever he was in town. Copies of some of his most famous works along with letters from the ruling Royal family addressed to him are on display.

ⓐ Rue de Chapitre 31 ⓣ 02 521 1383 ⓛ 10.00–12.00, 14.00–17.00 Tues–Sun ⓜ Metro: St-Guidon. Admission charge

Musée Horta

The noted art nouveau architect Victor Horta completed this home and studio in 1901. While the exterior is impressive, it's what's inside that counts. Every detail is flawless right down to the door handles. Visit on a weekday to avoid the crowds.
ⓐ Rue Américaine 25 ⓣ 02 543 0490 ⓦ www.hortamuseum.be ⓛ 14.00–17.30 Tues–Sun ⓜ Trams: 81, 82, 91, 92; Bus: 54. Admission charge

Musée Magritte

Magritte painted many of his works in the living room at the rear of this home. The museum now holds many of the artist's personal effects and letters.
ⓐ Rue Esseghem 135 ⓣ 02 428 2626
ⓦ www.magrittemuseum.be ⓛ 10.00–18.00 Wed–Sun
ⓜ Metro: Bockstael. Admission charge

Musée de la Résistance

The Belgian war resistance is honoured by this museum consisting of documents that chronicle its years of struggle.
ⓐ Rue Van Lint 14 ⓣ 02 522 4041 ⓛ 09.00–12.00, 13.00–16.00 Mon, Tues, Thur & Fri ⓜ Metro: Clemenceau

Musée Royal de l'Afrique Centrale

After decades of poor funding and politically incorrect displays, this museum dedicated to the history and culture of Belgium's former African colonies is finally being dragged into the modern age. Displays include archival notes taken from the files of the explorer Henry Stanley and a famous crocodile gallery that remains in the same form as its original 1910 setup. A major renovation of all the rooms is currently underway with completion set for some time in 2010.

ⓐ Chaussée de Louvain 13 ⓣ 02 769 5211
ⓦ www.africamuseum.be ⓛ 10.00–17.00 Tues–Fri, 10.00–18.00 Sat & Sun ⓝ Tram: 44. Admission charge

Musée Royal de l'Armée et d'Histoire Militaire
You'd expect a museum dedicated to the military to be pretty good in a country that has been fought over so many times – and you'd be right. Recently renovated, the room featuring aircraft from the two world wars is particularly interesting.

ⓐ Parc du Cinquantenaire 3 ⓣ 02 737 7811 ⓦ www.klm-mra.be
ⓛ 09.00–16.45 Tues–Sun ⓝ Metro: Mérode

Musées Royaux d'Art et d'Histoire
This large museum boasts a vast collection of antiquities from various historic global empires. While there aren't any real standout items, the sheer number of pieces is enough to warrant a visit.

ⓐ Parc du Cinquantenaire 10 ⓣ 02 741 7211 ⓦ www.kmkg-mrah.be
ⓛ 09.30–17.00 Tues–Fri, 10.00–17.00 Sat & Sun ⓦ Metro: Mérode

Musée du Transport Urbain Bruxellois
Visit this museum for a glimpse of the various methods of transport that once helped Brussels' residents travel across the

city. The restored trams and buses date back to 1869.
Alternatively, take a ride on one yourself by boarding the
old-fashioned tram that travels between the Parc du
Cinquantenaire and Tervueren.

ⓐ Avenue de Tervueren 364 ① 02 515 3108 ⓦ www.mtub.be
🕔 13.30–19.00 Sat & Sun, Apr–Oct. Admission charge

Musée Wiertz
Back in his day (1805–65), the artist Antoine Wiertz was a legend
in his own mind. Famous for painting massive biblical and
mythical scenes, he convinced the Belgian government to
purchase him a house and studio in return for inheriting his
works after his death. This museum is the end result.

ⓐ Rue Vautier 62 ① 02 648 1718 ⓦ www.fine-arts-museum.be
🕔 10.00–12.00, 13.00–17.00 Tues–Fri & every 2nd Sat & Sun
Ⓝ Metro: Trône

RETAIL THERAPY

Shopping streets & markets
Outside of the Petit Ring, you'll find both the ultimate in luxury
and fresh and funky street markets. For the big designer names,
look to Avenue Louise and the Boulevard de Waterloo where
you'll find Chanel, Gucci and Bulgari (among others). Mid-range
labels can be found on the Avenue de la Toison d'Or where high
street names are in abundance dotted throughout the galleries
that run off the main street. For ethnic finds and foods, look on
the Chaussée de Wavre, which runs parallel to Avenue Louise.
Meanwhile, bohemian and unique boutiques can be found on

Rue St Boniface. Finally, Rue du Bailli is the place to go for shoes, chain stores and chic cafés.

TAKING A BREAK

Café Belga £ ❶ An outdoor patio and sleek looks draw a crowd of artsy and wealthy media types. While it's more expensive than average, the interiors will make you feel like you're part of the cool club. ⓐ Place Eugene Flagey-Plein 18 ❶ 02 640 3508 ⓛ 09.30–14.00 Mon–Thur & Sun, 09.30–03.00 Fri & Sat ⓝ Bus: 71

Kafeineio £ ❷ Crowds flock to this buffet mezze bar with more than 50 hot and cold Mediterranean dishes to choose from. ⓐ Rue Stevin 134 ❶ 02 231 5555 ⓛ 09.00–01.00 Mon–Sat, 10.00–01.00 Sun ⓝ Metro: Schuman

AFTER DARK

Restaurants
Aux Milles et Une Nuits £–££ ❸ Camp and kitsch don't even begin to describe this Tunisian restaurant designed to look like a Bedouin tent. Surprisingly, the food is mouth-wateringly good with service to match. ⓐ Rue de Moscou 7 ❶ 02 537 4127 ⓦ www.aux-mille-et-une-nuits.be ⓛ 12.00–15.00, 18.00–23.30 Mon–Sat ⓝ Metro: Parvis de St-Gilles

L'Elément Terre ££ ❹ This venerable vegetarian establishment is one of the best in town. It features intriguing combinations and the finest in fresh organic ingredients. If you're willing to dabble, go for the discovery plate and have a little taste of everything. ⓐ Chaussée de Waterloo ⓣ 02 649 3727 ⓛ 12.00–14.30, 19.00–22.30 Tues–Fri, 19.00–22.30 Sat ⓝ Trams: 91, 92

Chez Marie ££–£££ ❺ Once a neighbourhood establishment, this French restaurant is now one of the hardest to get a table at – and all due to a single Michelin star. Interiors are cosy with fresh ingredients ensuring that everything is packed with flavour without getting too heavy. ⓐ Rue Alphonse de Witte 40 ⓣ 02 644 3031 ⓛ 12.00–14.15, 19.30–22.30 Tues–Fri, 19.30–22.30 Sat ⓝ Trams: 81, 82; Bus: 71

La Porte des Indes £££ ❻ If you thought the UK had a lock on great Indian restaurants, then you'd be mistaken. This classy establishment takes the cuisine to another level and features dishes you won't find at your local takeaway. Southern Indian cuisine is the speciality, but you'll have to spend a lot for the privilege. ⓐ Avenue Louise 455 ⓣ 02 647 8651 ⓦ www.laportedesindes.com ⓛ 12.00–14.30, 19.00–22.30 Mon–Thur, 12.00–14.30, 19.00–23.00 Fri & Sat, 19.00–22.30 Sun ⓝ Trams: 93, 94

Restaurant Bruneau £££ ❼ Restaurant Bruneau has two Michelin stars, and is an essential stop for fans of food. While it's far from the city centre, it's worth the trek. However, you might need a mortgage to afford the menu, which features dishes that cost anything from €40–€100 per course. ⓐ Avenue Broustin 75 ⓣ 02 427 6978 ⓦ www.bruneau.be ⓛ 12.00–14.00, 19.00–22.00 Mon, Thur–Sun ⓝ Metro: Simonis

Bars, clubs & discos

Fat Boys Mix with the expats at the popular sports bar hangout. So if you're missing the Premiership scores, or Ashes recaps, you know where to go. ⓐ Place du Luxembourg 5 ⓣ 02 511 3266 ⓦ www.fatboys-be.com ⓛ 11.00–late ⓝ Metro: Trône

L'Horloge du Sud Caribbean rums, live African music, R 'n' B dance nights – it's all here at this great bar in the heart of the Ixelles African community. You can even nibble on fantastic African/Belgian fusion cuisine. ⓐ Rue du Trône 141 ⓣ 02 512 1864 ⓦ www.horlogedusud.be ⓛ 11.00–01.00 Mon–Fri, 17.00–01.00 Sat & Sun ⓝ Metro: Trône

Cinemas & theatres

Théâtre 140 Physical theatre is the speciality of this innovative company under the direction of Jo Dekmine – a man who has been on the local scene for decades and worked with many artists of high calibre including Jacques Brel, Serge Gainsbourg and Pink Floyd. ⓐ Avenue Eugéne Plasky 140 ⓣ 02 733 9708 ⓦ www.theatre140.be ⓛ Box office: 12.00–18.00 Mon–Fri ⓝ Metro: Diamant

Théâtre de la Toison d'Or Wild and crazy revue-style comedy is what to expect at this venue specialising in satire. ⓐ Galeries de la Toison d'Or 396 ⓣ 02 510 0510 ⓦ www.theatredelatoisondor.be ⓛ Box office: 10.00–16.00 Mon, 10.00–18.00 Tues–Fri, 14.00–18.00 Sat ⓝ Metro: Porte de Namur

---

▶ *Book a tour of the Stella Artois building*

Antwerp

For great designer shopping, a peek inside the high-stakes world of the diamond industry, stunning art collections, capital clubbing and hip neighbourhoods in the form of the transformed waterfront warehouse district of Het Eilandje, Antwerp can't be beat. Go for a day or spend an even longer period in this city that Rubens once called home.

GETTING THERE

Four trains an hour make the journey between Antwerp and Brussels, taking 40 minutes to reach their destination. Alternatively, it's a quick 30–45 minute drive along the A12 or E19/A1 motorways.

SIGHTS & ATTRACTIONS

Sint Carolus Borromeuskerk

At the height of the Counter Reformation, the Jesuits built this church to honour the leader of the movement, the Archbishop of Milan. Rubens and students painted 39 ceiling paintings to decorate the interior. Unfortunately, a fire destroyed them all in 1718. Despite this incident, the church's beauty remained and the façade is still a highlight in this city of spectacular architecture.

ⓐ Hendrik Conscienceplein 6 ⓒ 03 272 2 023 ⓛ 10.00–12.30, 14.00–17.00 Mon–Sat

Grote Markt

Brussels may boast the Grand Place, but Antwerp rivals the capital city in terms of stunning squares in the form of Grote Markt. The spiritual heart of the city, the square offers up the most important architecture and historical buildings in Antwerp.

ⓐ Grote Markt

🔺 *Antwerp's Grote Markt rivals Brussels' Grand Place*

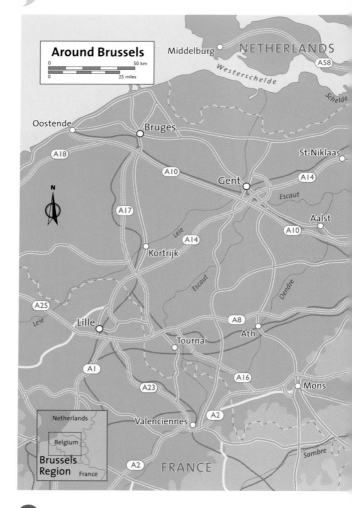

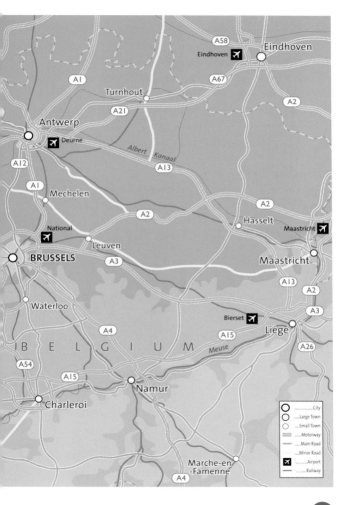

Onze-Lieve-Vrouwekathedral

This church is the largest Gothic church in the Low Countries and continues to dominate Antwerp's skyline. Despite the beauty of the interiors, it is the artwork that draws the crowds, including four large works by Rubens.

ⓐ Handschoenmarkt ⓣ 03 213 9940 ⓦ www.dekathedraal.be
ⓛ 10.00–17.00 Mon–Fri, 10.00–15.00 Sat, 13.00–16.00 Sun.
Admission charge

Rubenshuis

Antwerp's favourite son, the painter Rubens, bought this house in 1610 and used it as his studio until the day of his death. Step

⬤ *Onze-Lieve-Vrouwekathedral can be seen from far outside the city*

inside for a peek into what 17th-century Belgian life was like.
ⓐ Wapper 9–11 ⓣ 03 201 1555 ⓛ 10.00–17.00 Tues–Sun.
Admission charge

Sint-Pauluskerk

This church boasts the richest art collection in Antwerp. While
its original Gothic architecture has been somewhat obscured by
more recent baroque additions, the interior remains inspiring.
Highlights include works by Rubens and Van Dyck.
ⓐ Nosestraat ⓣ 03 232 3267 ⓛ 14.00–17.00 May–Sept

Stadhuis

Considered by many to be a symbol of the city, Stadhuis is
actually Antwerp's celebrated town hall built in the
Flemish–Italian Renaissance style. Both the exterior and the
interiors are impressive.
ⓐ Grote Markt ⓣ 03 220 8 020 ⓦ www.antwerpen.be ⓛ Tours:
14.00 Mon–Thur

Vlaeykensang

Go behind the gate at No. 16 Oude Koornmarkt to find this maze
of alleys dating back to the 16th century and you'll experience a
quiet square of contemplation away from the hordes.

CULTURE

Klank van de Stad

Formerly the city's meat market, this museum is the latest
addition to Antwerp's cultural scene. Occasional concerts and

vast collections of music and musical instruments chronicle the history and development of 'City Sounds'.

ⓐ Vleeshouwersstraat 38–40 ⓣ 03 233 6404 ⓛ 10.00–17.00 Tues–Sun

Koninklijk Museum voor Schone Kunsten Antwerpen

One of the most important collections in Europe with around 7,000 works. Highlights include pieces by Van Eyck, Breughel the Younger, Magritte and Rubens.

ⓐ Leopold de Waelplaats 2 ⓣ 03 238 7809 ⓛ 10.00–17.00 Tues–Sat, 10.00–18.00 Sun. Admission charge

Mayer van den Bergh Museum

A wealthy merchant compiled this collection of art treasures from the Low Countries. Masterpieces include works by Breughel the Elder along with priceless tapestries, sculptures and examples of stained glass.

ⓐ Lange Gasthuisstraat 19 ⓣ 03 232 4237 ⓛ 10.00–17.00 Tues–Sun. Admission charge

Middelheimmuseum

Technically located in the suburbs, this museum is worth paying the cab fare if you have an interest in sculpture. As the museum is open air, it is a popular place for families, weekend picnics and impromptu sporting matches. Pieces are of a high standard, including works from Rodin, Moore and Calder.

ⓐ Middelheimlaan 61 ⓣ 03 827 1534 ⓛ 10.00–21.00 Tues–Sun, June & July; 10.00–20.00 Tues–Sun, May & Aug; 10.00–19.00 Apr & Sept; 10.00–17.00 Tues–Sun, Oct–Mar

MoMu (Mode Museum)

This museum, the newest in the city, is dedicated to fashion and is probably the most dynamic museum in Antwerp (if not Europe). The permanent collection dedicated to chronicling the history of fashion is remarkable, but it is the innovative temporary exhibits that draw the masses. ⓐ Nationalestraat 28 ⓣ 03 470 2770 ⓦ www.momu.be ⓛ 10.00–17.00 Tues–Sun, 10.00–21.00 1st Thur of month

⬥ MoMu – Antwerp's innovative fashion museum

MuHKA

Once a grain silo, the Museum van Hendendaagse Kunst Antwerpen (or MuHKA) exhibits art from the 1970s onwards. This brief places it at the cutting edge of the art world and its reputation among those in the know is extremely high. The permanent collection of 700 works is rarely displayed in favour of radical temporary exhibitions. Both Belgian and international artists are supported and represented. Those with children should head straight to the first floor 'MUST for Kids' section, which is packed with toys and games inspired by art.

ⓐ Leuvenstraat 32 ⓣ 03 206 9999 ⓦ www.mukha.be
ⓛ 10.00–17.00 Tues–Sun

Plantin-Moretus Museum

It may sound boring, but this museum chronicling Flemish printing practices from the 15th–18th centuries is actually a real find. Many printers during this period worked at home in order to create works for their private library – so not only do you get a lesson in bookmaking, but also you get to learn more about the elite lifestyles of the period.

ⓐ Vrijdagmarkt 22–23 ⓣ 03 221 1450 ⓛ 10.00–17.00 Tues–Sun

Provinciaal Diamantmuseum

Three floors of the rock that's a girl's best friend. This interactive museum chronicles the journey of diamonds from rough stone to polished treasure.

ⓐ Koningin Astridplein 19–23 ⓣ 03 202 4890
ⓦ www.diamantmuseum.be ⓛ 10.00–19.00 Nov–Apr; 10.00–18.00 May–Oct. Admission charge

RETAIL THERAPY

Shopping streets & markets

Antwerp has been known as a high fashion destination ever since the famous Antwerp Six designers dominated London Fashion Week in the late 1980s. Today, names like Dries Van Noten, Ann Demeulemeester, Martin Margiela, Raf Simons, Dirk Bikkembergs and Wim Neels are splashed across the pages of luxury magazines on a regular basis.

Pick up a few designer pieces by wandering the streets of Antwerp's two hippest neighbourhoods: Het Eilandje and Het Zuid. Alternatively, do as the locals do and shop 'The Meir' at weekends when this becomes *the* place to see and be seen.

TAKING A BREAK

Grand Café Horta £ This café, located in the art nouveau masterpiece Horta Complex, is a great place to try some Belgian specialities. The perfect place to combine both visual and taste sensations while exploring the neighbourhood. **ⓐ** Hopland 2 **ⓣ** 03 232 7213 **ⓦ** www.grandcafehorta.be **ⓛ** 11.00–23.00 Mon–Fri, 11.00–24.00 Sat & Sun

AFTER DARK

Restaurants

Den Rooden Hoed £–££ Dating from 1750, this restaurant is the oldest in Antwerp. The cuisine, while never overwhelmingly good, is always solid. And the service is

very welcoming. The 16th-century wine cellar has recently been restored, making it a great place for wine connoisseurs. ⓐ Oude Koornmarkt 25 ⓣ 03 233 2844 ⓛ 12.00–14.30, 18.00–23.00

Broers van Julienne ££ Vegetarians will love this meat-free establishment with a Middle Eastern twist. ⓐ Kasteelpleinstraat 45–47 ⓣ 03 232 0203 ⓛ 12.00–22.30 Mon–Sat, 18.00–22.30 Sun

Caribbean Inn ££ Go through the medieval door and enter the West Indies with all the colour and delight you might expect. Jerk chicken and lobster *reggae* style are two of the can't miss faves. ⓐ Korte Nieuwstraat 22 ⓣ 03 231 0377 ⓦ www.caribbeaninn.be ⓛ 12.00–14.30, 17.30–23.00 Wed–Sun

Het Pomphuis £££ For a true blow-out meal, go straight to this converted art nouveau pumping station. While it's a little out of the way – you'll need to take a taxi to get there – the waterside views more than make up for the inconvenience. Resembling a brasserie, you might think French cuisine would be on the menu, but the selection is actually Pacific Rim inspired. ⓐ Siberiastraat z/n ⓣ 03 770 8625 ⓛ 11.00–14.30, 18.00–23.00 Mon–Fri, 11.00–23.00 Sat & Sun

Huis de Colvenier £££ This landmark establishment is truly one of the top spots in town in which to bag a table. Seriously fine French cuisine is what's on offer in the romantic salons. ⓐ Sint-Antoniusstraat 8 ⓣ 03 226 6573 ⓛ 12.00–15.00, 19.00–22.00 Tues–Fri, 19.00–22.00 Sat

Bars, clubs & discos

Café D'Anvers First it was a church. Then it was a cinema. Today, it's a deep house club. Around since 1991, it's a solid favourite with locals looking for uplifting beats. ❷ Verversui 15 ❶ 03 226 3870 Ⓦ www.cafe-d-anvers.com 🕐 23.00–07.00 Fri & Sat

Den Engel Easily Antwerp's most famous bar, this institution on Grote Markt only closes once the last customer leaves, so it can be open days on end considering the support of its character-filled regular clientele. A great place for a pre-club tipple or a post-big-night wind-down. ❷ Grote Markt 3 🕐 09.00–late

Elfde Gebod Early in the evening, the bridge and tunnel crowd call this bar home. Tour groups are often dropped off to admire the wacky architecture made to resemble a medieval church – with a few modern touches. As the evening progresses, the posers leave and the fashionable locals move in. ❷ Torfbrug 10B ❶ 03 289 3466 🕐 18.00–late

Fill Collins Club/Red & Blue The most debauched club in Belgium. Fridays are mixed, Saturdays as gay as a trip to San Francisco. Grace Jones once legendarily drove a stretch limo through the crowd of clubbers on the dance floor. ❷ Lange Schipperkapelstraat 11–13 ❶ 03 213 0555 🕐 23.00–late Fri, 23.00–07.00 Sat

Velvet Lounge Modelled on the Buddha Bar in Paris, this late-night chillout spot is ultra-hip and usually packed. Patrons are often dressed to the nines. ❷ Luikstraat 6 ❶ 03 237 3978 Ⓦ www.velvetlounge.be 🕐 18.00–late

Cinemas & theatres

Bourlaschouwburg The Bourla theatre was built in the 1830s as a centre for theatre and opera. A narrow escape from complete destruction eventually resulted in total renovation, completed in 1993 when Antwerp became the European Capital of Culture.  Komedieplaats 18 ☎ 03 231 0750

Kladaradatsch! Cartoon's Situated directly opposite the Steen, this cinema hosts the best of alternative cinema. The coffee isn't bad either.  Kaastraat 4–6 ☎ 03 232 9632

Sint-Augustinuskerk This deconsecrated church now offers a packed schedule of concerts, cultural events and exhibitions.  Kammenstraat 73 ☎ 03 202 4660

ACCOMMODATION

Hotel Florida £–££ The rooms may be impersonal, but you can't beat the price. The breakfast buffet is extremely filling.  De Keyserlei 59 ☎ 03 232 1443 🌐 www.hotelflorida.be

T'Elzenveld ££ Housed in the medieval buildings of a former hospital, this peaceful hotel offers period furniture in a garden setting.  Lange Gasthuisstraat 45 ☎ 03 2 02 7770 🌐 www.elzenveld.be

Hotel Villa Mozart £££ Country cute in the centre of old town. A nice place for romantics looking for somewhere cosy yet convenient.  Handschoenmarkt 3 ☎ 03 231 3031

Waterloo & Leuven

WATERLOO

The great battle at Waterloo changed the course of European history and destroyed the illustrious career of the great Napoléon. Thousands of visitors descend on the fields to the south of the town every year in order to witness the location that played a crucial role in the downfall of an Emperor.

A visit to the site invariably begins at the informative visitors' centre, where you can purchase entry tickets to the various locations of interest. An audiovisual presentation of the tactics involved in the battle is included in the cost of admission and well worth watching if you want to get an idea of the scale of the fighting.

❶ These days, the town of Waterloo may not be much to look at, acting as little more than a suburb of Brussels. However, this is set to change by 2008 as the local government is hoping to erase the *frites* stands and tatty souvenir shops in favour of a restored collection of 19th-century buildings, scale models and 3D films in order to make the destination more informative and up-market.

Waterloo Visitors' Centre ❸ Route du Lion 254, Braine l'Alleud ❶ 02 385 1912 Ⓦ www.culture-espaces.com/waterloo Ⓛ 09.30–18.30 Apr–Sept; 09.30–17.30 Oct; 09.30–16.00 Nov–Feb; 10.00–17.00 Mar. Admission charge

GETTING THERE

From Brussels, it's a 50-minute journey by bus from Place Rouppe to Waterloo. Buses run at half-hour intervals.

Alternatively, take one of the frequent commuter train services from the Gare du Midi. Journey time is 15 minutes.

SIGHTS & ATTRACTIONS

Butte de Lion
Erected by the Dutch ten years after the battle, this pyramid of 226 steps crowned by a lion provides stunning views over the famous battlefield.

ⓐ Route du Lion 252–254 ⓣ 02 385 1912 ⓦ www.culture-espaces.com/waterloo ⓛ 09.30–18.30 Apr–Sept; 09.30–17.30 Oct; 09.30–16.00 Nov–Feb; 10.00–17.00 Mar. Admission charge

Champ de Bataille
The Champ de Bataille is the actual battlefield on which the battle was played out. Located south of the actual town of Waterloo, these rye fields were stained red with the blood of French, British and Prussian soldiers on 18 June 1815 when the British, under the leadership of the Duke of Wellington, were attacked by Napoléon's army. More than 48,000 people died during the course of the battle, especially in skirmishes around the fortified farms of La Sainte Haye, Papelotte and Hougoumont. Every five years, the Battle of Waterloo is re-enacted featuring uniformed participants from around the world. The event happens on the Sunday closest to the battle's anniversary, with the next re-enactment scheduled for 2010.

ⓐ Route du Lion 252–254 ⓣ 02 385 1912 ⓦ www.culture-espaces.com/waterloo ⓛ 09.30–18.30 Apr–Sept; 09.30–17.30 Oct; 09.30–16.00 Nov–Feb; 10.00–17.00 Mar. Admission charge

Panorama de la Bataille

Created in 1912, this circular painting of the charge of the French cavalry is actually quite breathtaking. The artist's use of perspective and realism seems to take you onto the battlefield. Listen closely and you might even hear the cannons.

ⓐ Route du Lion 252–254 ⓣ 02 385 1912 ⓦ www.culture-espaces.com/waterloo ⓛ 09.30–18.30 Apr–Sept; 09.30–17.30 Oct; 09.30–16.00 Nov–Feb; 10.00–17.00 Mar. Admission charge

● *The lion memorial watches over the Champ de Bataille*

CULTURE

Musée Wellington

This former inn was the Duke of Wellington's headquarters during the fighting. Today, visitors will find displays that chronicle the events that occurred during the 100 days leading up to the Battle of Waterloo, plus maps and models of the battle itself. There are also a few items and souvenirs commemorating Wellington's victory.

ⓐ Chaussée de Bruxelles 147 ❶ 02 354 7806 ❻ 09.30–18.30 Apr–Oct; 10.30–17.30 Nov–Mar. Admission charge

Le Quartier Général de Napoléon (Napoléon's Last Headquarters, formerly the Musée du Caillou)

Packed with souvenirs and images of Napoléon, this museum located south of the battlefield in the town of Genappe contains the room where the formidable French Emperor spent his last evening before the battle that resulted in his demise. Displayed in the room are some of his personal effects and a number of objects found on the field.

ⓐ Chaussée de Bruxelles 66 ❶ 02 384 2424 ❻ 10.30–18.30 Apr–Sept; 13.00–17.00 Nov–Mar. Admission charge

TAKING A BREAK

Les 65 Colonnes £ Simple, yet popular brasserie serving seafood specialities and quality *steak frites*. Ample windows and bright interiors offer a warm welcome on even the most overcast days.

ⓐ Chaussée de Bruxelles 389 ❶ 02 351 5929 ❻ 11.00–23.00 daily

AFTER DARK

Restaurants

L'Amusoir ££–£££ Filling yet well-prepared Belgian dishes and succulent filet mignon with a variety of sauces draw the numerous punters to this popular steakhouse in the centre of town. While the white-washed building may look old and a little uncared for from the outside, the meals served up inside are sure to please. ⓐ Chaussée de Bruxelles 121 ⓣ 02 353 0336 ⓛ 12.30–15.00, 18.00–22.30

La Maison du Seigneur £££ Classy, family owned and operated restaurant serving fine French cuisine in a converted farmhouse. Menus are seasonal using only the best local ingredients. The terrace offers great views on warm summer evenings.
ⓐ Chaussée de Tervuren 389 ⓣ 02 354 0750 ⓛ 18.30–22.00 Wed–Sun, closed Feb and last 2 wks of Aug

ACCOMMODATION

Hotel le Côté Vert ££ There aren't many quality places to stay in Waterloo. This comfortable, simple hotel is one of the better ones. Expect cleanliness and a warm welcome. ⓐ Route du Lion 367 ⓣ 02 387 0060

LEUVEN

Which came first? The students or the beer? In this historic
town no one is really sure, as this university centre has been
known for both for centuries. This is Belgium's Oxford
equivalent dotted with bicycles, picturesque lanes and
dominated by the massive Interbrew brewery. For a drinking
tour of the country, you couldn't choose a better location.

GETTING THERE

Five trains an hour depart Brussels for Leuven. The journey time
is approximately 35 minutes. Alternatively, take the E40/A3
motorway east directly to the town.

SIGHTS & ATTRACTIONS

Grote Markt

Leuven's main square, like most major Belgian cities, is its heart.
Here is where you will find the treasures of the city's
architecture, including the Stadhuis (City Hall).

Sint-Pieterskerk

It may not be the prettiest church in Belgium, but Sint-
Pieterskerk is fascinating for architecture fans due to the fact
that it is essentially a failed project. Work on the church began
in the early 15th century and continued for more than 100 years
until locals decided to pull down some of the Romanesque
towers in order to accommodate a new plan designed by the
architect Joos Matsys. When it was discovered that the

foundations were too weak, the project was abandoned and the end result is what you see today. So if you think the exterior looks a little off, you wouldn't be mistaken. The towers were capped, creating an asymmetric look that jars slightly from what the eye is trained to appreciate.

ⓐ Grote Markt ⓣ 016 226 906 ⓛ 10.00–17.00 Mon–Sat, 14.00–17.00 Sun, closed mid-Dec–mid-Jan. Admission charge

Stadhuis

Leuven's Stadhuis (City Hall) is a masterpiece of Gothic architecture complete with all the ornate flamboyance one would expect from the period. Completed in 1469, it has survived

● Sint-Pieterskerk is interesting partly for its imperfections

a lot during its 500-plus years of existence, including drastic fires and a bomb explosion at its doors in 1944 at the height of World War II. Tours are available in Flemish and English.
ⓐ Grote Markt 9 ⓣ 016 211 540 ⓛ Tours: Mon–Fri 11.00 and 15.00, Sat & Sun 15.00, Apr–Sept; 15.00 daily, Oct–Mar

Stella Artois

Worship at the brewery that brought the world Stella Artois. A facility has been churning out beer on these grounds since 1366, but the drink we all know and love wasn't introduced until 1926. Reservations fill up fast so it is best to book well in advance.
ⓐ Vaartkom 33 ⓣ 016 247 111. ⓛ Tours: by reservation only 10.00, 13.30 & 15.00 weekdays. Admission charge

CULTURE

Museum Vander Kelen-Mertens

Pleasant enough museum with a wealth of porcelain plus collections of minor paintings and stained glass to highlight the fashions of the 16th century. ⓐ Savoyestraat 6 ⓣ 016 226 906 ⓛ 10.00–17.00 Tues–Sat, 14.00–17.00 Sun. Admission charge

RETAIL THERAPY

Shopping streets & markets

Brusselsestraat market If it's Saturday and you're an early riser, then make a beeline for the farmers' market on Brusselsestraat. Pick up fresh produce, cheeses, meats and local delicacies while you enjoy the lively atmosphere. ⓛ 09.00–12.00 Sat

TAKING A BREAK

Ombre ou Soleil Mediterranean brasserie-style dining that's good for a light lunch or quiet meal away from the masses. Fish and meat specialities are served in a sun-filled space. ⓐ Muntstraat 20 ⓣ 016 225 187 ⓛ 12.00–15.00, 18.30–22.00 Mon–Fri, 18.30–22.00 Sat

AFTER DARK

Restaurants

Belle Epoque £££ For special occasions, you can't beat the fine dining served up by house chef Ludo Tubée – especially during summer months when the open-air courtyard fills with local and visiting foodies. If you plan to stop by during the weekend, then be warned that advance reservations are a must. ⓐ Bondgenotenlaan 94 ⓣ 016 223 389 ⓛ 12.30–15.30, 18.30–23.00, closed mid-July–mid-Aug

Oestarbar £££ Many locals consider this place the best in town if you're hankering for fish or seafood. Unsurprisingly, oysters are the house speciality. In winter, an open log fire will warm your toes. ⓐ Muntstraat 23 ⓣ 016 202 838 ⓛ 12.00–15.00, 18.00–22.30 Tues–Sun

De Troubadour £££ This restaurant is where the locals go when they're looking for something special. Noted for its grilled meats and fish. ⓐ Tiensestraat 32 ⓣ 016 225 065 ⓛ 19.00–22.30 Wed, 12.00–15.00, 19.00–22.30 Thur–Sun

Bars, clubs & discos

Domus More a café/bar than an actual club, this rustic drinking spot adjoins the Domus brewery and is famous for its honey beer. The kind of place to go to for a late evening of slow drinking with friends. ⓐ Tiensestraat 8 ⓣ 016 201 149 ⓦ www.domusleuven.be ⓛ 09.00–01.00 Tues–Thur & Sun, 09.00–02.00 Fri & Sat

Silo Club As a university town, Leuven has its fair share of clubs. Situated in a former warehouse, the Silo Club is one of Belgium's best. ⓐ Vaartkom 39 ⓣ 016 237 252 ⓦ www.silo.be ⓛ 23.00–late Thur–Sun

ACCOMMODATION

Jeff's Guesthouse £–££ Italian-style restaurant and hotel with rooms that overlook the historic square on which it is situated. ⓐ Kortestraat 2 ⓣ 016 238 780

Theater Hotel ££–£££ Contemporary 21-room property with an adjoining art gallery. The buffet breakfast is well worth waking up for. ⓐ Bondgenotenlaan 20 ⓣ 016 222 819 ⓦ www.theaterhotel.be

Het Klooster £££ Splash out on this 16th-century country house with its modern rooms and luxurious amenities. ⓐ Predikherenstraat 22 ⓣ 016 213 141 ⓦ www.hetklooster.com

○ *Flume fun at the Bruparck swimming pool*

Directory

GETTING THERE

By air

For a short stay, those coming from the UK can fly to Brussels from a number of regional airports across the UK. Brussels' Zaventem International Airport is located approximately 14 km (9 miles) northeast of the city centre. Those choosing to fly with Ryanair will land at Brussels South International Airport in Charleroi, situated 55 km (34 miles) away. The average flying time from London is 1 hour. See also page 50 for more details on airports.

Many people are aware that air travel emits CO_2, which contributes to climate change. You may be interested in the possibility of lessening the environmental impact of your flight through the charity Climate Care, which offsets your CO_2 by funding environmental projects around the world.

Climate care Ⓦ www.climatecare.org

By rail

Travelling by rail is easy from the UK, and it provides the chance to see something of the countryside en route. The most common way is on Eurostar, which has nine departures a day (seven at weekends) between London's Waterloo International station and Brussels. The total journey time is approximately 2 hours 20 minutes.

Eurostar reservations (UK) Ⓣ 08705 186 186
Ⓦ www.eurostar.com

ℹ The monthly *Thomas Cook European Rail Timetable* has up-to-date schedules for European international and domestic train services. ℹ (UK) 01733 416 477; (USA) 1 800 322 3834
Ⓦ www.thomascookpublishing.com

By road

The Belgian motorway system is well integrated in the European motorway network. The easiest motorway to use is the E40/A10 if travelling from Ostend or the E40/A18, connecting with the E40/A10 if arriving by Eurotunnel into France. Driving in Belgium can be challenging as streets tend to be narrow and riddled with potholes once you leave the motorway. Congestion can sometimes be a problem, especially during traditional rush hours. One law to be aware of is the *priorité à droite* rule, which forces all cars to give way to any vehicle on the right – even on major roads. Trams always have right of way.
ℹ Try to avoid arriving or departing during rush hours, which extend between 06.30–09.30 and 16.00–19.00.
ℹ Belgian drivers are known to be aggressive and the one-way street system is cause for confusion.

By bus

Long-distance buses connect Brussels with most other European countries. From London by Eurolines, the fastest direct journey time is about seven hours depending on connections.

Eurolines Ⓦ www.eurolines.co.uk

ENTRY FORMALITIES

Visitors to Belgium who are citizens of the UK, Ireland, Australia, the USA, Canada or New Zealand will need a passport but not a visa for stays of up to three months. South African nationals do require a visa.

ⓘ If you are travelling from other countries, you may need a visa; it is best to check before you leave home.

Customs

There are no customs controls at borders for visitors from EU countries. Visitors from EU countries can bring in, or take out, goods without restrictions on quantity or value, as long as these goods are for personal use only. For visitors from outside the EU most personal effects and the following items are duty free: a portable typewriter, one video camera or two still cameras with ten rolls of film each, a portable radio, a tape recorder and a laptop computer provided they show signs of use; 400 cigarettes or 50 cigars or 250 g of tobacco; 2 litres of wine or 1 litre of liquor per person over 17 years old; fishing gear; one bicycle; skis; tennis or squash racquets; and golf clubs.

ⓘ As entry requirements and customs regulations are subject to change, you should always check the current situation with your local travel agent, airline, or a Belgian embassy or consulate before you leave.

MONEY

The currency in Belgium is the euro. If you are coming from another country in the EU that uses the euro currency, you will not need to change money. A euro is divided into 100 cents.

Currency denominations are: 50 euros, 20 euros, 10 euros, 5 euros, 2 euros, 1 euro, 50 cents, 20 cents, 10 cents, 5 cents and 1 cent. You can withdraw money using ATMs at many Belgian banks. The most widely accepted credit cards are Mastercard, American Express and Visa. Diners Club cards are less commonly permitted. ❶ Many smaller businesses, including some restaurants, taverns, smaller hotels and most market stalls do not accept credit card payment. This is especially true outside Brussels and the main tourist destinations. It is advisable always to carry a small amount of cash to cover your day's purchases.

HEALTH, SAFETY & CRIME

It is not necessary to take any special health precautions while travelling in Belgium. Tap water is safe to drink, but do not drink any water from surrounding lakes or rivers as the region is not known for its commitment to environmentalism. Many Belgians prefer bottled mineral water. *Pharmacies/apotheeks* (or 'pharmacies') are marked by a large green cross. Belgian pharmacists are always well stocked and staff can provide expert advice.

The standard of Belgian health care is good, but it is not free. In most cases your travel insurance should provide the coverage you need. A European Health Insurance Card (EHIC) – which replaced the E111 form – entitles you to free or cost-reduced medical treatment in EU countries.

As in any other big cities, crime is a fact of life in Brussels. Petty theft (bag-snatching, pick-pocketing) is the most common form of trouble for tourists. However, you are unlikely to experience violence or assault.

🛈 Always lock your car, and never leave valuables lying visibly in it.

🛈 Strolling around the inner city at night is fairly safe, but avoid dimly lit streets. Your hotel can advise you about particular areas to avoid.

🛈 When using public transport or walking on the street, carry your wallet in your front pocket, keep bags closed at all times, never leave valuables on the ground when you are seated at a table, and always wear camera bags and purses crossed over your chest.

For details of emergency numbers, refer to the 'Emergencies' section on page 138.

OPENING HOURS

Most businesses open 09.00–18.00 Monday–Friday. Department stores sometimes stay open until 21.00 on Fridays, while smaller boutiques actually close early on the same day. Generally, stores do not open on Sundays or public holidays. Banks open at 09.00 and close between 15.00 and 17.00 Monday–Friday. Cultural institutions close for one day each week – usually Mondays. Standard hours are 09.00–17.00. Only the biggest and most popular sights remain open seven days a week.

Usual post office opening hours are 08.00–19.00 Monday–Friday and 09.30–15.00 Saturday. The exception is the central post office on Groenplaats, which has slightly restricted hours.

TOILETS

At airports, railway stations and major tourist points, you should not have a problem finding toilets. Belgians have stocked their cities with loos – and most are sparklingly clean. Most locals, when pressed, resort to using facilities at cafés, restaurants and bars, though it is expected that you leave a tip of between 10 cents and 50 cents in the white dish that you will invariably find just inside the entrance.

❶ Be warned: many of the public facilities are unisex.

CHILDREN

Belgium is generally a child-friendly place and no special health precautions need be taken for children. Most restaurants welcome children, some even having play corners or outdoor playgrounds for the kids. There is usually a kids' menu with portions to go with the normal menu. If you ask, the staff will often be able to supply your children with pencils and paper at the table. Nappies and other baby articles are readily obtained from supermarkets or *pharmacies/apotheeks*.

Below are three child-friendly venues you should make a beeline for if you are looking for somewhere to keep the tots occupied.

Musée des Enfants Interactive children's museum in the heart of Ixelles. After a day of shopping the markets, bring the kids here and let them play with the puzzles, paints, modelling clay and adventure playground. Try to avoid it on Sundays when it's absolutely packed. ❷ Rue du Bourgmestre 15 ❶ 02 640 0107 ❶ www.museedesenfants.be ❶ 14.00–17.30 Wed, Sat, Sun, school holidays ❶ Tram: 23, 90; Bus: 71. Admission charge

Bruparck Attraction and theme park at the base of the Atomium. Rides include a giant Ferris wheel, plus a cinema complex and water slides. Bring patience and lots of cash.

ⓐ Avenue du Football 1 ☎ 02 478 0550 ⓦ www.bruparck.com
🕐 Park opens 09.30 from mid-Mar–Sept, 10.00 from Oct–early Jan,
closed mid-Jan–mid-Mar; park closes between 17.00 and 22.00
depending on season, so call ahead for details ⓜ Metro: Heysel

Scientastic Museum Interactive science museum with
workshops and experiments kids can try out. Factsheets are
available in English. ⓐ Underground level 1, Bourse, Boulevard
Anspach ☎ 02 732 1336 ⓦ www.scientastic.com 🕐 14.00–17.30
Sat, Sun, school holidays ⓜ Metro: Bourse

COMMUNICATIONS
Phones
Coin-operated public phones are rare; far more common are
card-operated phones. Telephone cards can be bought at any
post office and some shops (e.g. bookshops or kiosks at railway

DIALLING CODES
When making an international call, dial the international
code you require and drop the initial zero of the area code
you are ringing. The international dialling code for calls
from Belgium to Australia is 00 61, to the UK 00 44, to the
Irish Republic 00 353, to South Africa 00 27, to New
Zealand 00 64, and to the USA and Canada 001.

The code for dialling Belgium from abroad, after the
access code (00 in most countries) is 32. To call Antwerp from
within Belgium dial 03 and then the number, unless calling
from Antwerp itself when you can drop the 03 pre-code.

stations). A display shows how much credit is left. Instructions on how to use public telephones are written in English in phone booths for international calls. Otherwise, lift up the receiver, insert the telephone card and dial the number.

Post

Postal services are quick and efficient. Stamps can be bought at the numerous post offices or from automatic vending machines. Post boxes are yellow. Letters less than 20 g to Belgium and EU countries cost 59 cents or 84 cents to all other destinations.

Central Post Office ⓐ Centre Monnaie, Place de la Monnaie
ⓣ 02 226 2111 ⓒ 08.00–19.00 Mon–Fri, 09.00–15.00 Sat
Ⓝ Metro: De Brouckère

Internet

Internet access is hard to come by around the city. If you're desperate for access, try heading for Ixelles, which has a few call centre Internet cafés charging about €1.50 per half-hour.

One recommended location is **Intercall Telecom**
ⓐ Chaussée de Warre 69 ⓣ 02 502 5696 ⓒ 09.00–24.00
Ⓝ Metro: Trône

ELECTRICITY

The standard electrical current is 220 volts. Two-pin adaptors can be purchased at most electrical shops.

TRAVELLERS WITH DISABILITIES

Facilities for visitors with disabilities are generally quite good in Belgium. These facilities are usually indicated by a blue pictogram of a person in a wheelchair. In all towns and cities there are reserved car parks for wheelchair users. Motorway service stops, airports and main railway stations always have suitable toilet facilities. Most trains also have toilets accessible for wheelchairs. Furthermore, many cinemas, theatres, museums and public buildings are accessible. Many hotels in Brussels are wheelchair-friendly. However, you will need to make a request when you book. For further advice on facilities in Brussels, contact the tourist office.

🛈 One word of warning for wheelchair users: many of Belgium's streets are cobblestoned.

A useful source of advice when in Belgium is **Vlaamse Federatie voor Gehandicapten** ⓐ Sint-Jansstraat 32–38, Brussels B1000 ⓣ 02 515 0262 ⓦ www.vfg.be

USEFUL WEBSITES

ⓦ www.sath.org (US-based site)
ⓦ www.access-able.com (general advice on worldwide travel)

FURTHER INFORMATION

There are two excellent tourist offices that serve Brussels: one deals with queries about the city; the other deals with queries about the province. Maps and information are eagerly distributed by the friendly and efficient English-speaking staff.

Brussels International Tourism & Congress ⓐ Hôtel de Ville, Grand Place ⓣ 02 513 8940 ⓦ www.bitc.be ⓛ 09.00–18.00 daily (summer); 09.00–18.00 Mon–Sat (winter) ⓝ Metro: Gare Centrale

Office de Promotion du Tourisme Wallonie-Bruxelles
ⓐ Rue du Marché aux Herbes 63 ⓣ 02 504 0390
ⓦ www.belgium-tourism.net ⓛ 09.00–18.00 daily (summer); 09.00–18.00 Mon–Fri, 09.00–13.00, 14.00–18.00 Sat, 09.00–13.00 Sun (winter) ⓝ Metro: Gare Centrale

FURTHER READING

Tintin by Hergé. Read any of the illustrated books from the Tintin series to discover the colourful comic traditions of the country.
The Professor by Charlotte Brontë. This first novel by Brontë is set in Brussels, yet struggled to find a publisher. Not as strong as her later works, it is still an interesting chronicle of Belgian society life.
Amoenitates Belgicae by Charles Baudelaire. These scathing poems attacking Belgium and its residents might put you off a visit, but their humour and passion can't be denied.
Vanity Fair by William Makepeace Thackeray. While not solely devoted to Belgium, the middle of the novel features delicious descriptions of society life in Brussels immediately prior to the Battle of Waterloo.
A Tall Man in a Low Land by Harry Pearson. Witty travel writing providing entertaining takes on modern Belgian life and etiquette.
The Dutch Revolt by Geoffrey Parker. Excellent historical chronicle of the happenings that led to the end of the Spanish empire in the Low Countries during the 16th century.

Emergencies

EMERGENCY NUMBERS
Ambulance 100
Fire brigade 100
Police 101

MEDICAL EMERGENCIES
Most doctors in Belgium speak at least basic English. All will be expensive, so make sure you have a European Health Insurance Card (if you are from the EU) and/or private travel insurance. Prescription and non-prescription drugs (including aspirin) are only sold at pharmacies. Most pharmacies open 09.00–18.00 Mon–Fri and 09.30–15.00 Sat.

Hospitals
Hôpital Brugmann ⓐ Place van Gehuchten 4 ① 2 477 2010 Ⓝ Metro: Houba-Brugmann
Hôpital Erasme ⓐ Route de Lennik 808 ① 02 555 3111 Ⓝ Metro: Erasme
Hôpital St-Pierre ⓐ Rue Haute 26 ① 02 535 3111 Ⓝ Metro: Porte de Hal

POLICE
If you lose anything or suspect that it has been stolen, then go straight to the nearest police station. While there, you will need to make a statement and fill in the required forms for insurance purposes. The central police station is located at ⓐ Rue du Marché au Charbon 30 ① 02 279 7979

CONSULATES & EMBASSIES

Australian Embassy ⓐ Rue Guimard 6-8 ⓣ 02 286 0500
ⓦ www.austemb.be ⓛ 08.30–17.00 Mon–Fri

British Embassy ⓐ Rue d'Arlon 85 ⓣ 02 287 6211 ⓦ www.british-embassy.be ⓛ 09.00–17.30 Mon–Fri

Irish Embassy ⓐ Rue Wiertz 50, Brussels ⓣ 02 235 6671
ⓦ www.irlgov.ie/iveagh ⓛ 10.00–13.00 Mon–Fri

New Zealand Embassy ⓐ Second floor, Square de Meeûs 1,
Brussels ⓣ 02 512 1040 ⓦ www.nzembassy.com/belgium
ⓛ 09.00–13.00, 14.00–17.30 Mon–Fri

Republic of South Africa Embassy ⓐ Mercator Building, Rue de la
Loi 26, Brussels ⓣ 02 285 2200 ⓦ www.southafrica.be
ⓛ 08.30–17.00 Mon–Fri

US Embassy ⓐ Boulevard du Régent, Brussels ⓣ 02 508 2111
ⓦ www.usembassy.be ⓛ 09.00–18.00 Mon–Fri

EMERGENCY PHRASES

Help! Au secours! *Ossercoor!*

Stop! Stop! *Stop!*

Fire! Au feu! *Oh fur!*

Call an ambulance/a doctor/the police/the fire service!
Appelez une ambulance/un médecin/la police/les pompiers!
*Ahperleh ewn ahngbewlahngss/ang medesang/lah poleess/leh
pompeeyeh!*

SPOT A CITY IN SECONDS

This great range of pocket city guides will have you in the know in no time. Lightweight and packed with detail on the most important things from shopping and sights to non-stop nightlife, they knock spots off chunkier, clunkier versions. Titles include:

Amsterdam	Bratislava	Glasgow	Madrid	Salzburg
Antwerp	Bruges	Gothenburg	Marrakech	Sarajevo
Athens	Brussels	Granada	Milan	Seville
Barcelona	Bucharest	Hamburg	Monte Carlo	Sofia
Belfast	Budapest	Hanover	Munich	Stockholm
Belgrade	Cardiff	Helsinki	Naples	Strasbourg
Berlin	Cologne	Hong Kong	New York	St Petersburg
Bilbao	Copenhagen	Istanbul	Nice	Tallinn
Bologna	Cork	Kiev	Oslo	Turin
	Dubai	Krakow	Palermo	Valencia
	Dublin	Leipzig	Palma	Venice
	Dubrovnik	Lille	Paris	Verona
	Dusseldorf	Lisbon	Prague	Vienna
	Edinburgh	Ljubljana	Porto	Vilnius
	Florence	London	Reykjavik	Warsaw
	Frankfurt	Lyon	Riga	Zagreb
	Gdansk		Rome	Zurich
	Geneva			
	Genoa			

The publishers would like to thank the following for supplying the copyright photographs for this book: Pictures Colour Library page 47; Recyclart page 34; Visit Flanders pages 36 & 49; all the rest Neil Setchfield.

Copy editor: Sandra Stafford
Proofreader: Rebecca McKie

Send your thoughts to
books@thomascook.com

- Found a great bar, club, shop or must-see sight that we don't feature?

- Like to tip us off about any information that needs updating?

- Want to tell us what you love about this handy little guidebook and more importantly how we can make it even handier?

Then here's your chance to tell all! Send us ideas, discoveries and recommendations today and then look out for your valuable input in the next edition of this title. As an extra 'thank you' from Thomas Cook Publishing, you'll be automatically entered into our exciting prize draw.

Send an email to the above address (stating the book's title) or write to: CitySpots Project Editor, Thomas Cook Publishing, PO Box 227, The Thomas Cook Business Park, Unit 18, Coningsby Road, Peterborough PE3 8SB, UK.